Yoel Sheridan was born and educated in London, England and immigrated to Israel in 1973. He is the author of *From Here to Obscurity* published in 2001, an historical novel that deals with the now lost vibrant Yiddish-speaking community of the East End of London. and *Gold Ducats and Devilry Afoot, An Historical Narrative of The Trials and Tribulations of Henry Simons, A Polish Jew in Mid-eighteenth Century England.* published in 2012. His *Essay on Jews, Feudalism and the Magna Carta Mediaeval Myth Management and Modern Mismanagement* was published in November 2017. Curiosity has been and remains his driving force.

To the fighters of antisemitism

Yoel Sheridan

ANTISEMITISM AND THE 1753 *JEW LAW* CONTROVERSY

AUSTIN MACAULEY PUBLISHERS™

LONDON • CAMBRIDGE • NEW YORK • SHARJAH

A CIP catalogue record for this title is available from the British Library.

ISBN 9781398442276 (Paperback)
ISBN 9781398442283 (ePub e-book)

www.austinmacauley.com

First Published 2022
Austin Macauley Publishers Ltd®
1 Canada Square
Canary Wharf
London
E14 5AA

Without the encouragement and patient support of my wife Tova over the years, the critical assistance of my son Kevin, and the help of librarians in the British Library and the Hasafran Listserv of the Association of Jewish Libraries, this book would never have been completed.

Table of Contents

Preface	**11**
Introduction	**19**
Chapter 1	**23**

*Parliament And the Parlous Legal Position
of Jews Prior To June 1753*

Chapter 2	**28**

*Analyses of, and Comments on, Selected
Published Works*

Chapter 3	**53**

*Prynne, Cromwell and the Return of the
Jews to England*

Chapter 4	**57**

*King George II (1683–1760) – King of England
from 1727 to 1760*

Chapter 5	**65**

*The Jewish Community in Mid-Eighteenth
Century London*

Chapter 6	**74**

Pamphlets

Chapter 7	**93**

Antisemitism

Preface

The misnamed Jewish Naturalization Act of 1753, that became known pejoratively as the *Jew Law* or *Jew Bill,* was enacted in June and repealed in December 1753. The very same English Parliamentarians, who earlier in the year passed the Bill, repealed it before the year was out. This simple fact is enough to arouse one's curiosity and raise the question *'why'*? Why pass the Bill and then almost immediately repeal it?

A wide-ranging study was required as most historians have concentrated on the immediate causes of the repeal that will now be re-examined. Relatively, little has been written as to why the Bill was passed, and no real attempt has been made to explain why the Bill was proposed in the first place; especially, when all the antisemitic arguments that precipitated its repeal were already well-known to the proposers, and nothing has been written about the King's influence. There is the mistaken belief that this controversy was just a spasmodic interlude, after which antisemitism was absent.

I have examined previous works critically and taken issue with various opinions and conclusions which required the study of other works and periods to reach a more authentic assessment of the controversy.

This book has developed from the narrower subject of the controversy over the Act itself to include the everlasting question of endemic antisemitism in Britain. Previous writers have not dealt sufficiently with this, and I have given it the weight I think it deserves.

My original interest arose from simple curiosity as to why the *Jew Law* was enacted and then repealed within six months, but it soon became clear to me that the repeal was due to virulent antisemitism being used to launch a damaging political attack on the Government of the day.

The *Bill* was misnamed as it never did propose general naturalization, it merely provided a method for foreign-born individuals professing the Jewish faith to take the oaths when applying for naturalization, without adding the words upon *the true faith of a Christian,* which was a fundamental requirement, originally enacted to ensure the supremacy of the Protestant Church of England over the Papacy. The Government said that the Bill was innocuous as it simply provided a method whereby any rich foreign Jew, who had resided in England for three years, could apply for naturalization through an expensive process that also ensured the worthiness of the applicant to become a British citizen. Applicants had also to prove that they were of the Jewish faith. There was no question of general naturalization and importantly, Parliament remained free to approve or reject any application at will.

However, none of this allayed the fears generated by the opposition's virulent antisemitic campaign to repeal the Act and influence the upcoming general election that was due the following year. They totally misrepresented the Bill by calling it a General Naturalization Bill for all Jews far and wide, including British residents, and claiming that it offered preference over foreign Protestants.

Thomas W. Perry, Todd M. Endelman, James Shapiro, and Nicholas Rogers have written much on this subject. Each has his own slant on the reasons for the *uproar* that preceded the repeal of the *Jew Law*. Perry suggests that it was a political ploy due to upcoming elections, Endelman argues that it was part of the much broader anti-Jewish sentiment prevalent in English society, while Shapiro says it was the need to define what is an Englishman. Rogers leans towards Perry. None pay much attention as to why the law was introduced in the first place. None deal seriously with the parliamentary debates or the King's influence. Perry rightly recognises the political nature of the opposition, but, surprisingly, gives little or no weight to the antisemitic element, of which there is much evidence.

The *uproar* was, in fact, the unleashing of a long litany of lies against the Jews, and a catalogue of their alleged past, and possible future, calumnies, and here we have the first and prime example of antisemitism being used as a trigger to launch a damaging political attack on the Government of the day. It was used effectively as a weapon to rouse the irrational fears and hatred of the masses. The hubbub and threat of violence created panic in the governing Whig party, whose leadership decided that they had better repeal the Act if they were to restore calm.

The discourse included economic and civil arguments. Those in favour of the Bill argued that the strength of a nation depended on the number of its inhabitants, that competition and anti-monopolism should be supported, that the State should have no legitimate interest in examining the religious beliefs of its citizens, that royal feudal slavery of the Jews had been swept away with other feudal practices by the *Glorious Revolution*, that Jews were men like other men and non-Christians could be good citizens in a Christian state, and that Jews were useful, as they were experienced importers and exporters. However, no one argued that Jews should be given equal political rights. Those against the Bill feared that the participation of additional Jewish merchants in existing trade would decrease the English merchants' share, with some adding, especially that as the Jews are subtle people, they would deprive English merchants of any profits they would otherwise gain.

Nevertheless, the question remains, what induced the wily politicians to introduce the Bill in the first place? *Nicholas Rogers* says that the concessions in the Bill were modest and the *Gentlemen's Magazine* claimed that the Bill was intended for "private purposes". Endelman claims that the Bill was introduced by the Prime Minister and his brother, as a favour to Joseph Salvador and other Jews, a small band of financiers, who had supported the policies of the Government. But it is still difficult to understand why the wily governing triumvirate of the Prime Minister, Henry Pelham; his brother, the Duke of Newcastle, Secretary of State, Thomas Pelham-Holles; and the Lord High Chancellor, Philip Yorke, would have taken such a politically dangerous course to introduce the Bill as a Government measure, when they were fully aware of the endemic explosive antisemitism extant at the time. No one dealt with the possibility of the King's intervention, which is considered herein, in the chapter on his life.

An important objection to the *Jew Law* was related to the questionable rights of Jews to hold property. This was subject to much argument. There were extensive, inconclusive legal discussions in the contemporary publications and debates about the rights of Jews to reside, and own land and property. Any claims that Jews had such rights were strongly countered by claims that any rights that may have been given were conditional and could always be revoked at the King's pleasure. The objectors opined that Christianity was endangered if Jews were permitted to hold church property, and they insisted that history had shown that Jews had no unconditional rights of residence. Jews had indeed, over the years, faced restrictions, not only in England, but also in Spain, Portugal, Paris, Russia, Bohemia, Austria, Hungary, Italy, Turkey and many other countries.

The promoters of the Bill erred heavily by including the word *Jew* in its title, when, as Endelman pointed out, the mere use of this monosyllable carried with it enough unfavourable connotations to raise prejudice to a frenzy, whereby it could be believed that St. Paul's Cathedral was in danger of being turned into a Synagogue, and that mass circumcision was on the cards. Thomas Herring, the then Archbishop of Canterbury (1747-1757), complained that, "this ridiculous prejudice is being trumpeted all over England, in which I am not so much concerned for its influence on the next election, as I am to see how easy it is to raise this foolish people to an inhuman and savage spirit". Lord Hardwicke wrote that the rage of the people was ungovernable, and the Earl of Granville observed during the repeal debate that the clamour was chiefly, if not entirely, owing to the Act happening, unluckily, to get a wrong title. The antagonists read much more into it, and one pamphleteer wrote knowingly, that the uproar "was not as a matter that regards the Jews only, but as it is a matter that concerns our own and Great Britain's welfare, we should endeavour to allay the present spirit lest bad consequences follow. It is ridiculous to imagine that the present ferment is raised only against the Jews".

Perry contends that there was an absence of violence against individual Jews or their property, which led him to believe that the uproar was political, and not antisemitic. However, there is clear evidence of the continuous threat of imminent violence and its effect on the stability of the Government. The threat was embodied in the passionate antisemitic clamour, that was instrumental in obtaining the repeal of the Bill. This is confirmed in the remarks of the Duke of Newcastle, when he said that no rich Jew "will choose to live in a country where he is likely to be the butt of popular malice and resentment", and by Lord Chancellor Hardwicke, who was convinced that the ill humour of the people would have broken out into violence, if it had not been for their hope that the law would be repealed as soon as Parliament met again. And there was the openly antisemitic speech of the Earl of Egmont, at the end of the debate in April 1753, who mischaracterised the Bill and said, in terms that could only be interpreted as a clear threat, that "this is a Bill intended to Naturalize the Jews, or it is a Bill intending nothing". And that "the nation will see through this design, and by some means or other, I am confident, will defeat it". They will not agree to the "naturalization of that people, the very essence of whose character and religion consists in their abhorrence of Christianity, and rancour to the whole Christian race". The pamphleteer Philo Patriae was very concerned as to where antisemitic incitement might end. He wrote that some thousands of His Majesty's subjects were unjustly terrified, and he quoted Aesop; "*Said the frog to the boy,*" in the fable, *"what may be play to them, is death to others."*

The outbreak of pernicious antisemitism was not just a spasmodic interlude that came from nowhere when the Bill was passed, to die out immediately after the Bill was repealed. It was, in fact, a manifestation of the endemic Jew-hatred so openly exhibited in mediaeval England that had survived the 366 years between 1290 and 1656, during which, England was *Judenfrei.* Jews were considered infidels and could in no way be deemed natural-born English citizens. Proof is in the language of the debates, and in the many published pamphlets that contained the oft-repeated litany of ancient antisemitic lies and calumnies, in one form or another; as listed in William Prynne's 1655 publication, the Demurrer, that was against Cromwell's decision to allow Jews to return to England. These antisemitic views were carried well beyond 1753; and in 1848, when the naturalization debate was renewed, Barrister Egan decried those who mistakenly still held the view that all Jews were aliens or bondsmen of the Sovereign and, like the Turks and Infidels, were perpetual enemies of Christians.

Although the antisemitic hubbub receded after the repeal of the *Jew Law*, the antisemitic atmosphere continued. This is evidenced in the King's concern, expressed in a letter from the Duke of Devonshire to the leading Jewish financier, Gideon Samson, in 1758. The Duke wrote that the King had said to him that he should have no objection himself to oblige Samson with a Baronetcy, "but as you was not bred up in the religion of the country, he was afraid it would make a noise, and in a time of confusion & public distress, as the present is, he was afraid they would make an ill use of it". It is also clear from the security fears expressed in the contemporary records kept by the Jewish Community.

In Britain in 1753, Catholics were denied equal rights because they had demanded religious supremacy and threatened the throne, Christian Dissidents were denied equal rights because they threatened the religious supremacy and solidarity of the Church of England, and the Jews, who were loyal supporters of the King, were denied equal rights as a result of antisemitic clamour.

I cannot close without acknowledging the encouragement and patient support of my wife, Tova, over the years, the critical assistance of my son, Kevin, and the help of librarians in the British Library and the Hasafran Listserv of the Association of Jewish Libraries, without which this book would never have been completed.

I am confident that this book will explain the *Jew Law* controversy and will also expose the pernicious nature of antisemitism; and the damaging consequences to society as a whole, of failing to confront it wherever, whenever and in whatever form it appears. Antisemitism is a real threat to decent democratic society.

YS

Introduction

Britain has a long history of antisemitism. Its first blood libel, commonly known as the Murder of Little St. William of Norwich, dates back to 1144. Jews were falsely accused of torturing and killing a Christian child in order to use his blood to make Passover matzo. The Church claimed William as a holy martyr and set up a shrine for his remains. Copycat claims followed and shrines were dedicated in 1168 to St. Harold of Gloucester; in 1181, to St. Robert in Bury St. Edmonds; in 1183, to St. Adam in Bristol; and in 1255, to Little St. Hugh, who was buried as a martyr in Lincoln cathedral. In 1190, there was the infamous massacre of 150 Jews in York. These are but examples of the many violent, anti-Jewish outbreaks in towns across medieval England from which, the Jews were completely expelled in 1290.

Despite objections, Cromwell tacitly allowed Jews to resettle in England in 1655.

Much had changed in England between 1290, when the Jews were expelled, and the year 1753, when the misnamed Jewish Naturalization Act of 1753 was passed and repealed within six months. Twenty-two Kings had reigned, and the King on the throne of England in 1753 was George II. There had been four important political events that were later to affect the position of the Jews. Henry the Eighth broke with the Catholic Church in 1534, and established Protestantism in England. Charles the first was beheaded in 1649 and the Cromwellian Commonwealth ruled for following ten years. The Bill of Rights was signed in 1689, changing the balance of power to give more say to Parliament and less to the monarchy; and the political system had evolved from raw mediaeval feudalism to a (form of) representative parliamentary system, where members were elected to the House of Commons[1].

Buccaneering and pirating had evolved into commercial trading, and financial and commodity institutions had been established; and in 1720, the stock market faced its first major crisis when the *South Sea Bubble* burst. In 1752, the nation switched from the Julian calendar to the more accurate Gregorian calendar. This change applied to all His Majesty's Dominions and Countries in *Europe, Asia, Africa,* and *America,* belonging or subject to the Crown. Britain was well established around the world. The Preface to the Census Returns of 1851 indicated that the population of the whole of England and Wales was only 6,039,684 in 1750. The population of London was well below one million, Bristol was one of the larger English towns with a population of about one hundred thousand and there were, approximately, six thousand Jews in the country.

English national identity was in the process of development and, for many, a *Church of England-Protestant-Christian* identity was an essential part of having an English identity. The English language was still evolving and

---

[1] Voting rights were restricted to men and the House of Lords could overrule laws passed by the House of Commons.

Jonathan Swift, in 1712, felt that the language was in a chaotic state.[2] Samuel Johnson must have agreed, as his famous dictionary was published in 1755.

With the defeat of the Jacobite uprising in 1745, the Protestant Church of England had firmly established itself, but it remained strongly protectionist. Its worst enemy in 1753 was Catholicism, and *Jacobite* and *Papist* were loaded words in those times. The wars of succession in England were religious wars and many of the laws promulgated in Britain were basically designed to keep Catholicism at bay.

There were three oaths incumbent upon persons wishing to become citizens of Britain. Immigrants had to swear allegiance to the Crown, to the Protestant Church of England, and take the oath of abjuration upon *the true faith of a Christian*. These oaths were anti-Catholic in design, but they operated equally against Jewish and other non-Protestant religious sects, and against Protestant Dissenters and Quakers. The Toleration Act of 1689 made some concessions, but it was not until 1858 that oaths were finally amended to enable Catholics, Jews, Dissenters and others to become members of the British Parliament, hold official offices, buy property and to trade freely.

The parliamentary debates on the 1753 *Jew Bill* were long and heated. They, and the many lengthy contemporary pamphlets (equivalent of today's social media) provide ample material for studying the true nature of antisemitism. The term *antisemitism* was non-existent, until it was coined in 1879 by Wilhelm Marr, a German publicist. Prior to that date, there was no need for a euphemism to express Jew hatred. It was

---

[2] David Crystal, "Evolving English" British Library 2010, page 48.

openly expressed in Britain in 1753, with no laws to set limits to the form or manner of its expression.

Material critically examined to complete this book includes: books by *Thomas W. Perry, Todd M. Endelman, James Shapiro and Nicholas Rogers,* a review on the Status of the Jews in England from the time of the Normans by Barrister *Charles Egan*, biographies of George II by *Jeremy Black* and *Andrew C. Thompson, Hansard's* parliamentary debates, and various other books, pamphlets, articles, and documents relating to the Bill and its hasty repeal. This was needed to gain a broader view of the history of the Jews in England and the social and political conditions extant in mid-eighteenth-century England.

The *Jew Bill* was passed at the end of a spring parliamentary session, and in the summer recess that followed, there were extraordinary countrywide cries of outrage which expressed the unwarranted xenophobic and antisemitic fears of the public. The hubbub forced the Government to repeal the Act.

Questions remain and answers will be sought here.

Chapter 1

Parliament And the Parlous Legal Position of Jews Prior To June 1753

The Corporation Act of 1661 and *The Test Act of 1673*, both of which were repealed in 1828, required persons accepting an appointment or election to office, to take the sacrament according to the usage of the Church of England; thus, excluding Catholics, Protestant Dissenters and Jews, Quakers and adherents to the Church of Scotland [3] (mainly Presbyterians) from office and advancement.

The Revolution of 1688, traditionally referred to as the *Glorious Revolution*, and the *Bill of Rights* signed in January 1689, are generally seen as marking the emergence of Parliament as the supreme power, displacing the Monarch who no longer could claim the *divine right* of kings. He now derived his power from the representatives of the people, embodied in Parliament that ensured its own ultimate say in any power struggles by keeping control of the purse strings.

---

[3] Search out the Land S. J. and J.C. Godfrey-McGill-Queen's University Press 1995.

The Toleration Act of 1689, exempted Dissenters, who had taken the oaths of allegiance and supremacy, from certain penalties and restrictions of the earlier Test Act[4].

Parliament met every year from 1690, usually for several months at a time. In 1694, the maximum length of a parliament was set at three years by the Triennial Act. In 1716, this was changed to seven years by the Septennial Act[5]. Parliaments were divided into separate sessions, usually a year long. The office of Prime Minister evolved during the early part of the 18th century, when King George I ceased attending meetings of his ministers and it was left to the leading minister to act as Government Chief Executive. Sir Robert Walpole (1721–42) is considered to have been Britain's first prime minister. He was followed by Spenser Compton (1742–43) and Henry Pelham (1743–54).

It was King George the Second's Government under the leadership of Henry Pelham that passed and repealed the 1753 *Jew Law,* that was specifically designed for wealthy Jews, as the legal costs involved to apply for citizenship under the Act were very high. Poor Jews were already covered by the 1740 Plantation Law, which enabled them to obtain British citizenship if they worked for seven years in the Colonies.[6] Under the 1753 Law, Jews had to be resident in England for three years and prove that they were of the Jewish faith.

---

[4] Parts of this act were repealed by the Promissory Oaths Act 1871; the rest were repealed in the Statute Law (Repeals) Act 1969.

[5] The maximum of five years was introduced in 1911 under the Parliament Act, since when there have been further amendments.

[6] An attempt, during the 1753 Jew Law repeal debate, to exclude Jews from the 7-year rule, failed.

Foreign born Jews, non-citizens and non-denizens [7] were considered *Aliens* and subject to special taxes and trading and property-owning restrictions.

In June 1753, when the *Jew Law* was enacted, there were said to be some 6,000 to 8,000 Jews in Great Britain. They were immigrants, or off-springs of immigrants, who had come into England after 1655. Foreign-born Jews were designated as aliens. They could not become citizens because, in order to be naturalized, it was necessary to take the three oaths; swear allegiance to the Crown, to the Church and declare that the Protestant Church of England was supreme. The third oath, known as the oath of abjuration, contained the words *upon the true faith of a Christian*. The 1753 *Jew Law* allowed Jews to take the required oaths without the use of this phrase, however, no claims for citizenship by Jews were recorded in the six-month period that the law was in force. No explanation has been offered, but it may be assumed that the unsavoury political atmosphere probably acted as a deterrent. Aliens could not vote, hold office in municipalities nor other places of trust under the crown. They could not sit in parliament nor enter a university. They could not unconditionally own property or a British ship or take part in colonial trade and were subject to alien duties such as import levies and special port fees.

The legal status of the Jews in Britain was a matter of dispute, the underlying religious nature of which can be derived from these examples taken from the debates.

---

[7] A denizen is an alien admitted to residence in a country, with certain limited rights of citizenship.

Sir Edmund Isham said, "If we are still Christians, it must have some weight to observe that by the Bill, and by the doctrine lately broached by our lawyers that Jews born here may purchase and hold land estates, then we are giving the lie to all the prophecies in the New Testament, and endeavouring, as far as we can, to invalidate one of the strongest proofs of the Christian religion. By those prophecies, they are to remain dispersed: they are to remain without any fixed habitation, until they acknowledge Christ to be the Messiah, and then, they are to be gathered together from all corners of the earth, and to be restored to their native land."

Lord Dupplin said, "Children of aliens born in this kingdom know that their children born here will be deemed natural born subjects without any Naturalization Bill and may be entitled to the rights and privileges of Englishmen. If an alien should purchase real estate of any kind in this country, he cannot hold it, no, not for his life; for the moment he has purchased such an estate, it belongs to, and may be claimed by the crown: nay, he cannot hold a lease for years of any such estate, except only of a house for his habitation, in the case of his being a merchant, and even of such a house the lease goes to the crown upon his death." He quoted Sir William Blackstone[8] who wrote that "in order the better to secure the established church against perils from non-conformists of all denominations, infidels, Turks, Jews, heretics, papists and sectaries, there are, however, two bulwarks erected; called the Corporation and Test acts. By the former, of which no person can be legally elected to any office relating to the government of any city or corporation, unless, within a twelvemonth

---

[8] Sir William Blackstone's Commentaries on the Laws Page 373

before, he has received the sacrament of the Lord's supper according to the rites of the Church of England; and he is also enjoined to take the oaths of allegiance and supremacy at the same time that he takes the oath of office. The other, called the Test Act, directs all officers, civil and military, to take the oaths and make the declaration against transubstantiation,[9] in any of the King's courts, within six calendar months after their admission; and also, within the same time to receive the sacrament of the Lord's Supper according to the usage of the Church of England. This test having been removed in 1753, in favour of the Jews, was the next session of parliament restored again with much precipitation".

---

[9] Transubstantiation is the belief that the bread and wine given at Communion become the body and blood of Jesus Christ when they are blessed.

Chapter 2

Analyses of, and Comments on, Selected Published Works

Public Opinion, Propaganda and Politics in Eighteenth Century England—A Study of the Jew Bill of 1753, by Thomas W. Perry[10]

Perry's work is devoted entirely to the *Jew Bill*. It is detailed and valuable, and subsequent writers have relied heavily upon his research. He gives accurate and well-supported day by day (sometimes hour by hour) reports on the, pro and anti, speeches, petitions, writings, and developments that preceded the passing of the Bill, and then to the six months of clamour that led to its repeal. His assumptions and conclusions are, however, open to question.

He minimises the importance of the parliamentary debates, saying that "they must so often be taken with a grain of salt", even though the debates clearly reveal the attitudes of the Parliamentarians who enacted and repealed the Bill. He is in error when he assumes that the engine of antagonism to the Bill was only the longstanding general Tory and Whig

---

[10] Harvard University Press, Cambridge, Massachusetts, 1962.

doctrinal disagreement on immigration and naturalization, to the exclusion of endemic antisemitism that was inflamed by the pejorative characterisation of the Naturalization Act as the *Jew Bill*. Perry was wrong when he wrote in his preface that the word *'Jew'* used as an adjective did not then have the derogatory overtones that it had in the 1960s, especially as Jew hatred was openly expressed in the parliamentary debates and literature of the time. The pejorative connotation was always there.

Perry contends that the absence of violence against individual Jews or their property was the best evidence for the argument that the passions stirred up by the clamour, were largely intended to be directed against the Court (Whig) politicians rather than against the Jews, whereas the Duke of Newcastle said, in the November 1753 debate on the repeal, "This clamour might prevent many rich Jews from taking advantage of those laws we formerly had in favour of their naturalization, for no man (who can live quietly and securely, as a rich Jew, in most of our neighbouring countries) will choose to live in a country where he is likely to be the butt of popular malice and resentment." The Earl of Granville said that while the clamour raised against the Act had been pretty universal, he believed the cause was chiefly, if not entirely, owing to the Act happening unluckily to get a wrong title. If, instead of calling it an Act for permitting Jews to be naturalized, it had been entitled an Act to Prevent the Profanation of the Holy Sacrament of the Lord's Supper, no objection would have been made to it. Lord Chancellor Hardwicke also explained during the repeal debate, that he was convinced that the ill humour of the people would have broken out into violence, if it had not been for their hope that the Law would be repealed as soon as Parliament met. The absence of violence could also be attributed to the passing of the Riot and Gin Acts in 1714 and 1751 respectively. More importantly, Perry made no reference to the very belligerent and openly antisemitic speech of the Earl of Egmont at the end of the debate in April 1753, when the Bill was passed. The Earl mischaracterized the Bill and said, in terms that could only be interpreted as a clear threat as to the shape and nature of the future public outcry, "This Bill is a step to a general naturalization, which was very daringly attempted, but happily defeated, not above two years ago[11]. The same spirit now animates those, who moved you then to attempt that hateful measure: they dare not openly avow the same design, but they artfully endeavour to bring it about again by this means; knowing full well how strong this argument must be hereafter, when you have passed this Bill, what! will you, who have consented to naturalize even the Jews, and boggle at allowing the same privilege to foreign Protestants professing the Christian religion as you do yourselves? But the nation, Sir, will see through this design, and by some means or other, I am confident, will defeat it now, as they did then. I conclude with what I have been led to say upon naturalization in general, and upon this naturalization of the Jews in particular, with this common proverb that there is no rule without an exception, and that if ever there should be an exception to any general principle, it ought surely to be in the case of the naturalization of that people, the very essence of whose character and religion consists in their abhorrence of Christianity, and rancour to the whole Christian race."

---

[11] This refers to a 1751 Bill to naturalize foreign Protestants.

To support his theory that the controversy over the *Jew Bill* was exclusively the existence of a continuing doctrinal disagreement of many years, standing on the subject of immigration and naturalization policy and the vitality in the old two party divisions, Perry ignored the fact that antisemitism can be, and was, used as a political tool, and that there is no contradiction in admitting that it was an actively essential element in the political fight to repeal the *Jew Law*. James Shapiro in his book *Shakespeare and the Jews* does not accept Perry's view, and goes so far as to write, "For Perry, the Jew Bill was never about the Jews." In addition, an openly antisemitic pamphlet entitled *A Modest Apology*, begins by saying that the Bill is entirely of a religious nature, and that great pains have been taken to make one believe that trade was the principal end in view.

Perry does concede that there is a difference in tenor in the language used in the previous debates on earlier Bills, proposing the general naturalization of foreign Protestants that had been introduced by Mr Nugent in 1747 and 1751[12]. He notes the language differences[13] when explaining that the wording of the City's 1753 petition "was far more sweeping in its assertions and more immoderate in its language than any of the others on either side of the controversy. The others considered the Bill solely in an economic light; none of them so much as suggested that it had a religious or political aspect". He adds that while the City petition raised economic

---

[12] The Parliamentary History of England from the earliest period to 1803. Parliamentary Debates Vol. xiv, A.D. 1747–1753, Hansard 1813.

[13] Page 58.

objections, it did so only after expressing the petitioners' apprehensions that the Bill would tend greatly to the dishonour of the Christian religion and endanger "our excellent Constitution".

On December 4, 1747, an attempt to introduce a Bill for the Naturalization of Foreign Protestants was defeated by 187 to 103 votes. The arguments for and against the Bill were based upon cultural and economic arguments. Much was said about the effect immigration would have on the comparative wage levels, and the benefits that rich immigrants would have on expanding the economy. But the negative arguments won the day[14]. The Jews' request to be included in this Bill had been refused and there is no reference to them in the debate, which was conducted in calm parliamentary language, and not in the heated exchanges of the 1753 Debates. The vituperative language was reserved for the Jews.

Perry does not discuss the role, if any, of King George II.

****

The Status of the Jews of England from the Times of the Romans to the Reign of Her Majesty Queen Victoria by Charles Egan, Barrister. [15]

---

[14] The Parliamentary History of England from the earliest period to 1803. Parliamentary Debates Vol. xiv, A.D. 1747–1753, Hansard 1813.

[15] London 1848. Part of the Parkes Collection. Southampton University.

In contrast to the dismissive approach of Perry, Egan feels that the repeal of the 1753 *Jew Law* was one of the most painful incidents in English constitutional history. The clamour it aroused was from disaffection clothed in superstition. Almost a century after the repeal of the *Jew Law*, the Prime Minister, Lord John Russell[16], had still to argue in Parliament that Jews born in England should be entitled to the honours and advantages which the British Constitution gave every Englishman, and that religious opinion of itself ought not to be a disqualification. Lord Russell explained that the laws requiring oaths to be taken *upon the true faith of a Christian* were intended against the Popish religion. This requirement also disqualified Protestant Dissenters and Jews. Laws passed in 1828 and 1829, removed all disabilities from Catholic and Protestant Dissenters, but not from the Jews who were still unjustly treated as aliens until 1858.

The question before the 1753 Parliament dealt with foreign-born Jews, whereas the 1847 debate concerned British-born Jews, but as far as the opposition was concerned, this was a distinction without a difference. Mr Macauley MP said that the English constitution was primarily a Christian constitution, and it was the first duty of Christian legislators to protect it from infidels. A Jew could not listen to the Christian form of prayer, they were a separate nation and creed, and as was stated in a speech by the Duke of Bedford in 1753, no Jew can be deemed a natural-born English citizen. It would not be right nor expedient to favour 30,000 or even 40,000 Jews, at the risk of exasperating three or four million English citizens. Lord Ashley disclaimed any antipathy to the

---

[16] Prime Minister of Great Britain in 1846–1852, and 1865–1866

Jews and maintained that the prejudices of 1847 had no connection with the personal hatred arising from the crucifixion nor with those prejudices that existed in 1753, but his opposition was based on a principle of religious truth. No advantage would be gained by removing the disabilities of the Jews, whilst it would occasion a great shock to thousands of honest and conscientious Christians. Mr G. Bankes supported Lord Ashley and expressed his horror at the possibility of seeing a Jew as Premier. Mr Law said that the admission of a Jew into Parliament would displace a Christian and make room for an infidel or an atheist. He considered this Act as more subversive of the best interest of this country than any measure yet proposed to Parliament and ominously warned Lord Russell that if the Act were passed, the people might demand something more than a repeal as they did in 1753. Mr Newdegate asserted that the wealth of one distinguished Jew had been liberally lavished to obtain petitions in favour of the Bill. He also insisted that the passing of the Bill would lead to a severance of the Church from the State and said that such a severance had led to the abolition of the French monarchy. Lord Drumlanrig reminded the House that Jews were unfortunately actuated by the love of money. Mr Horsman (who supported the Bill) said that the opposition's old cry that the Church was in danger had now been changed to Christianity being in danger. Mr Disraeli supported the Bill but said that he would prefer to retain the words on the true faith of a Christian, and to give special exemption to the Jews by a separate clause.

The House of Commons passed the Bill on May 4, 1848, with 234 for the Bill and 173 against. But on May 25, 1848, the House of Lords rejected the Bill with 163 against and only 128 for the Bill.

Objections were raised in the House of Lords. The Earl of Ellenborough could foresee political dangers arising from the national and social character of the Jews, who are citizens of the world rather than citizens of England. He called on the Lordships not to deprive themselves of heavenly aid by decreeing the desecration of Parliament and destruction of the Christian nature of the British Legislature. The Duke of Cambridge said he had the greatest respect for individuals of the Jewish persuasion, and he had never hesitated to assist Jews in obtaining privileges that he thought could be safely conceded to them, but as long as this country was a Christian country, it was impossible to admit Jews to sit in this Legislature. The Archbishop of Canterbury, Dr Bird Sumner, founded his objections on the peculiar character of the Jews and also the conscientious dislike and dread by a large class of persons, who considered it a sort of insult to the Christian religion. While the Earl of Winchelsea had the warmest feelings of charity towards members of the Jewish persuasion, he could not admit them into Parliament and what is more, he warned that if the Bill passed, the result would be that within a year, not one of the Bishops would have a seat in the House. The Bishop of Oxford said that the gulf between Christian and Jew was as wide as eternity itself. The Jews of England had no political rights and were here on condition that they should not have political privileges. This Bill, if passed, would lead to the separation of Church and State. The Earl of Desart said that if Jews were sincere in their religious opinions, then they must be anxious to destroy all Christian institutions. Lord Stanley was of the opinion that a sincere Jew must desire to see the Christian religion trodden in the dust. While Jews, particularly educated Jews, were conscientious, charitable, well-disposed and loyal, they could not be put on an equal footing with any Christian denomination or any other British subject. Practically, the Jews of this country were not of this country, but of a nation apart, they had the interests of the Jews, not British and not Christian interests. Viscount Canning noted that in contrast with 1753, there was an absence of public meetings against the current Bill.

Egan decries those who mistakenly still held the view that all Jews were aliens or bondsmen of the Sovereign, and like the Turks and Infidels, were perpetual enemies of Christians. He attempted to answer their assertion that the Jews had no fixed residence in any Christian country and lived in expectation of ultimately returning to Jerusalem.

Age-old antisemitic canards were still being openly repeated in the mid-nineteenth century England.

****

The Jews of Georgian England 1714–1830 by Todd M. Endelman.[17]

Todd Endelman's book was primarily written to show that the acculturation of Anglo-Jewry during the Georgian period moved at a more rapid pace than elsewhere in Europe. This against the widely held view that Moses Mendelsohn's intellectual revolution in Germany was the decisive event that spawned Jewish modernity in the West. He also claims that

---

[17] The University of Michigan Press, 1999 – Earlier versions exist.

Anglo-Jewry as a whole enjoyed a degree of toleration not to be found on the continent. There is no separate chapter dealing with the *Jew Law*, to which numerous references are made throughout the book.

Endelman explains that in 1753, the restrictionist economic views of the City were working against improving the status of the Jews, while the wealthy Sephardi merchants and brokers, led by Joseph Salvador, were seeking to free foreign-born Jews from discriminatory foreign commerce regulations that had remained in force, due to Cromwell's failure to gain public acceptance of Jewish resettlement. He says that the Bill was introduced by Prime Minister Henry Pelham and his brother, the Duke of Newcastle, as a favour to Salvador and other Jews, a small band of financiers, who had supported the policies of the Government.

He notes that the City merchants, represented in the Commons by Sir John Barnard, were quick to denounce the Bill as injurious to the interests of English commerce. Those merchants who traded with Portugal submitted a petition against the Bill. Their vehement protest had the support of the Lord Mayor and leading Aldermen, outweighing the counter petitions of merchants supporting the Ministry who maintained the Bill would increase the nation's trade. Endelman says that the objections of the City merchants were not exclusively economic, as they also expressed the fear that the Christian religion would be dishonoured and the Constitution endangered. Nevertheless, he maintains, the initial motive of the City opposition was economic.

He writes that liberal thought that disfavoured religious and other monopolies, potentially worked towards improving the position of the Jews. In particular, he refers to the Whig

Act of 1709 for the Naturalization of Foreign Protestants, which was repealed by the Tories after their electoral victory in 1710; and the reaction of the freethinker, John Toland (1670–1722), who in his 1714 publication *Reasons for Naturalizing the Jews in Great Britain and Ireland,* regretted that the Jews had not been included in the 1709 Bill. Toland believed in the force of numbers and that more immigration would increase economic activity, both in consumption and exports. Endelman refers to an anonymous pamphlet entitled *'The Expediency of a General Naturalization of Foreign Protestants and Others',* published in 1751 that repeated Toland's arguments and in addition, dismissed the charge that the Jews would work for less and take the bread out of the mouths of the poor.

Although Perry and others have reported the lack of violence against the Jews, Endelman writes that the harassment of Jewish street traders and itinerant pedlars was a frequent occurrence. They were molested, insulted, abused and refused board and lodging by innkeepers[18]. Specifically, he refers to the murder of Jonas Levi in November 1753, and to mob violence—though much later—that was reported on King George the third's birthday in 1763.

There is some discussion regarding the anti-Jewish vocabulary used in the anti-*Jew Bill* literature. Doubts are raised as to whether the epithets were derived from genuine religious zeal or just politically inspired. Perry has argued that most of the violent anti-Jewish language was of a political

---

[18] This is confirmed by the treatment, in 1751, of Henry Simons whose trials and tribulations are related in my book *Gold Ducats and Devilry Afoot.*

partisan nature, while Endelman concludes that it is a synthesis of the two positions.

Tracing the source of anti-Jewish sentiment is academic, the resultant antisemitism is a reality whatever the language and whatever form it takes. As Endelman says, "The mere use of the monosyllable *Jew* carried with it enough unfavourable connotations to raise prejudice to a frenzy, whereby it could be believed that St. Paul's Cathedral was in danger of being turned into a Synagogue and that mass circumcision was on the cards." Antisemitism was not restricted to the ignorant masses, as is revealed in the parliamentary debates. Medieval, negatively charged images of Jews had become part and parcel of England's cultural heritage. It was alleged that Jews would use their fortunes to gain control of the kingdom, they would buy up landed estates and carry elections and take over the courts, oppose and destroy Christians, guilty or innocent. Reports were printed in 1753, from an imaginary future 1853 Hebrew Magazine where a Bill for naturalizing Christians was thrown out of the Sanhedrin by a large majority.

While it was held that Jews were indistinguishable from Christian merchants or gentlemen, and that well-educated and well-to-do Portuguese Jews moved freely in Christian society, antisemites claimed that they could spot a Jew by the malignant blackness underneath his eyes or by his complexion, they had a Portuguese look.

No one argued that Jews should be given equal political rights.

Endelman does not discuss the role, if any, of King George II, indeed, when the King is mentioned, he is mistakenly referred to as his grandson George III.[19]

****

Shakespeare and the Jews by James Shapiro[20]

James Shapiro's book contains seven chapters. He writes in the introduction that the book is concerned with what Shakespeare (1564–1616) and his contemporaries thought about the Jews. However, it goes beyond the Bard's short life span to deal with the wider influence on later generations. Shakespeare's play, *The Merchant of Venice* that included the Jewish negative stereotype, *Shylock*, was published in 1600, when there was no Jewish community in England. The last chapter of Shapiro's book is devoted to *Shakespeare and the Jew Bill of 1753,* confirming that Shakespeare's influence, a century and a half after his death was still extant.

Shapiro gives only a few sentences to the details of *Jew Bill* itself, referring the reader to other historians for the facts of "this alien legislation". He does note, however, that in the six months between the introduction of the Bill and its repeal, more than sixty pamphlets, endless newspaper columns, various satiric illustrations, sermons and an assortment of related books had been printed, for and against, the *Jew Bill,* and that almost as rapidly, the controversy disappeared from print and public scrutiny once the Bill had been repealed. He

---

[19] This could just be a typing error.
[20] Columbia University Press 1996.

adds that historians have since puzzled over what the controversy was really about. As with other writers, Shapiro's main interest is not the Bill, but the public reaction that led to its repeal. There was little public interest when the Bill was introduced. In fact, there was no opposition in the House of Lords when the Bill was proposed on April 7, 1753 and the second reading of the Bill in the House of Commons on May 7, 1753 was carried by a comfortable majority of 95 to 16. More interest was engendered after petitions for and against the Bill, were presented during the May 22nd third reading, when a motion for adjournment was defeated by 96 to 55, after which the Bill was finally passed without further division.

Shapiro says that two broad explanations have been offered for the uproar concerning the Bill, and he offers a third; the need to define what is an Englishman? The first explanation maintains that the opposition provided an opportunity for Jew-baiting, a view supported by a number of Anglo-Jewish historians, and Shapiro admits that there is certainly enough evidence in the *Jew Bill* controversy of the crudest sort of racial (i.e. antisemitic) prejudice. He gives examples of this prejudice and quotes the work of Todd Endelman, who argues that what happened in 1753 was part of the much broader anti-Jewish sentiment prevalent in English society at that time. The opposing revisionist view, advanced by Perry, maintains that what was ultimately at stake was no more and no less than the political struggle in an election year between the Whigs (the Court Party) and the Tories (the City Party). Shapiro says that for Perry, the *Jew Bill* was never about the Jews, and that Perry's position has been supported and modified by recent scholars like Nicholas

Rogers, who nevertheless (according to Shapiro) was of the opinion that opposition in the provinces was derived from an ingrained antisemitism and xenophobia, while City opposition was directed at the Jewish merchants and the fear that their participation in available funds would increase as a result of naturalization. There was also the fear of massive immigration of foreign traffickers that would be detrimental to local traders and shopkeepers. Shapiro says that there are problems with both of these two main interpretations. He proposes instead that it was the need to define the question of what is an Englishman that was the underlying force pushing for repeal of the *Jew Law*. He suggests that the buried threat, occasioned by the naturalization of the Jews had to do with the surprising vulnerability of English social and religious identity at this time. If even a Jew could be English, what could one point to, that could be defined as Englishness?

Why Shapiro should be surprised is in itself surprising, as he is aware of the quite recent past English history, when the whole social and religious structure of England had been seriously threatened by the Jacobite uprising. An uprising that was supported, in July 1745, by the invasion of the Catholic Pretender Charles Edward Stuart (Bonny Prince Charlie), which was defeated at the battle of Culloden in April 1746. Shapiro chooses to ignore this influential piece of history, instead, he concentrates on showing how sixteenth century English ideas about the racial, national, and criminal nature of the Jews left their mark upon the debate.

Shapiro details the xenophobic and racial writings that were part of the general debate on the repeal of the *Jew Bill* in order to prove his point. However, the examples given are as much, or even more so, antisemitic as they are xenophobic.

He says that "early modern English attitudes toward the Jews informed Shakespeare's *The Merchant of Venice;* Jews were aliens, they were a separate nation, racially set apart, and, most ominously, they secretly desired to take the knife to Christians in order to circumcise or even castrate them" and that these stereotypes were dusted off and tried out again on the English public. He feels that the *Jew Bill* controversy should be placed within the broader context of eighty years of debate concerning immigration and naturalization, where the wider question of religious toleration had been vigorously fought. Toleration was seen as damaging religious conformity and the severing of the tight bond between the temporal and the spiritual, i.e. promoting the disestablishment of the Church of England. There was general antagonism to allowing Catholics, Christian Dissenters, Jews, Moslems and any other non-Christians to worship freely. The *Act of Toleration* passed in 1689, was the first successful attempt to break with the past regime of coercive religious conformity, but even the prime promoter of tolerance, the philosopher, John Locke, later replaced his call for the toleration of the Jews by his desire for their conversion. One of the movements supporting the acceptance of Jews into England, was the belief that they could then be converted to Christianity. A more strident Christian belief was that Jews were aliens and incapable of being anything else. On the other hand, Dissidents felt that it was wrong to restrict the rights of citizens because of their religion. Shapiro is of the opinion that what was at stake in the debates on the *Jew Bill*, as in previous immigration debates, was not the Jews themselves so much as the broader social principles embodied in accepting them into the social fabric. Despite his earlier caustic remark that for Perry, there were no Jews, he seems to be aligning himself with Perry's basic thesis. Shapiro uses many examples of unfavourable comparisons between Jews and English Christians, to support his view that the English were trying to define themselves by explaining what they certainly were not. In further support, he quotes other scholars of English nationalism and of the emergence of Englishness, who have maintained that the eighteenth century was the period in which 'a sense of British[21] national identity was forged'.

While this may well be true, it would seem to be a step too far to suggest that this was the real reason for the six-month uproar surrounding the *Jew Bill*.

Shakespeare's Shylock in The Merchant of Venice was a huge influence on British attitudes towards Jews. Although there were supposedly no Jews in England when the play was written, and the play is set in Venice, Italy, the Shylock stereotype of the Jew is neither Venetian nor Italian. Instead, as with all critical aspects of the Jews, it is universal. The play was normally staged at the beginning of the London autumn season, but it was not performed in the 1753 season. There is some controversy as to the reason for this censorship, some suggesting that it came from the Lord Chamberlain's office, whereas Shapiro shows evidence that it is more than likely a

---

[21] Ask an Englishman for his nationality and he will quite likely answer British while a Scotsman will answer Scots, the Welshman, Welsh and the Northern Irishman, Irish. All are British. The term British is often used in place of English. The context determines whether such juxtaposition is acceptable. Shapiro appears to use both terms synonymously here.

voluntary omission by the management of the Drury Lane theatre to avoid rowdiness that was likely to occur if the play was staged at the height of the *Jew Law* controversy. The following extract from Shapiro's book gives a telling example of how the play was used by opponents of the *Jew Bill*.

J.E. Gentleman, the author of 'Some Considerations on the Naturalization of the Jews' in the midst of a long diatribe against Jewish naturalization, turns to the matter of the Jews' 'exorbitant avarice'. The subject immediately put him in mind of a passage in *The Merchant of Venice* and he begins by citing Shylock's hatred of Antonio, "I hate him as a Christian." He then proceeds to quote at length from *The Merchant of Venice,* including lines in the trial scene where Shylock gloats over having been awarded a pound of Antonio's flesh. Shakespeare's play reveals just what kind of threat awaits the English if they naturalize the Jews. After three uninterrupted pages of quotation from Shakespeare's play, he demands of his readers: "And now, Englishmen and countrymen, judge ye, what advantage it can be to you to have these Jews naturalized! What can you get by them? They are all griping usurers. And what can they get out of you, but your very blood and vitals?"

The Shylock stereotype is derogatory, and it was used freely to attach a nefarious agenda to both Christian and Jewish promoters of the *Jew Law*.

Shapiro does not discuss the role, if any, of King George II.

****

Whigs and Cities, Popular Politics in the Age of Walpole and Pitt[22], London Politics from Walpole to Pitt; Patriotism & Independency in an Era of Commercial Imperialism 1738–1763[23] by Nicholas Rogers.

Rogers points out that while, in 1753, a handful of towns were dominated by landed grandees, the great majority were independent boroughs with active electorates and the City of London was politically autonomous. Government financing was by way of government loans, raised by a system of closed subscriptions in collaboration with prominent Dutch and Jewish financiers. City merchants and small rentiers led by Sir John Barnard, resented their exclusion. Prominent Sephardic Jews had by this time integrated into mainstream and social English life. They had adopted English habits and modes of dress and had mixed with the reigning Whig dynasties. Through the individual efforts of financial barons, such as Joseph Salvador and Gideon Samson, they had established important links with the Treasury. Nevertheless, they remained an identifiable ethnic and religious community and they suffered various legal and other restrictions, including being barred from becoming Freemen of the City and from holding shares in certain joint stock companies. They had gained a reputation for being shrewd speculators. Jewish immigrants were, however, handicapped in general trading, as they were regarded as aliens and subject to heavy port and custom duties. They could not own land except through the expensive process of endenization, and even then, their

---

[22] Clarendon Press, Oxford 1989.

[23] PhD dissertation, University of Toronto, 1975

foreign-born children could not inherit. They had hoped that their disproportionate financial support of the Government— they had supplied one quarter of the financing during the 1746 uprising—would hold them in good stead when seeking improved rights. But still in 1751, when Robert Nugent proposed his General Naturalization Bill for foreign Protestants, Jews were excluded. As Dutch, Huguenot and Jewish Merchants formed the mainstay of Whig moneyed interests in London, the *Jew Law* concessions could be seen to be for political services rendered, a bargain between the ruling dynasty and foreign-born Jews already living in England.

Two petitions sympathetic to the measure were tabled by 102 London merchants and traders, manufacturers and shipwrights in the woollen trade, while several City merchants in the Portuguese trade signed a petition against the Bill, and the London Evening Post published a series of articles on the dangers of promoting the Bill. The campaign against the Jews intensified during the summer. Fears were voiced that there would be a full-scale invasion of Jews, the Capital would become the New Jerusalem, and the Evening Post argued that within ten years, most of our tenants may have Jewish landlords and two thirds of our freeholders will be circumcised and forced to vote as ordered. All the latent prejudices came to the fore in writing, caricatures and violence. Rogers cites violent incidents including the burning of a Jew in effigy to illustrate the clamour against the *Jew Bill*. Jews were hooted, hunted, cuffed, pulled by the beard, spat upon and barbarously assaulted without protection from any passers-by. There was a persistent strain of antisemitism among the *menu peuple*[24] of the City of London, and in the parishes and suburbs throughout the first half of the 18th century. Commentators, Rogers writes, have ignored this substratum of bigotry. The Bishop of Norwich was openly insulted, as were the rest of his bench. The clergy in Oxford were worried and some MPs were facing difficulties with their constituents. Unrest had spread across the country, but the groundswell of opposition to the Bill lay principally in London. The suggestion that the uproar had been engineered, overlooks the rampant antisemitism of the metropolis; but there was a growing fear that the *Jew Bill* would be used against the Court (Whig) party in the upcoming political contests. Suspecting this, the Pelhams took steps to repeal the Act early in the next session. This gesture helped to placate the storm.

The 1754 election was fought principally on Jewish naturalization. It was won by the Whigs, but with a smaller majority. They did not do well in London. The absence of genuine party affiliations in the City and the underlying conservatism of the Livery Companies [25] were important factors, but they were overwhelmingly eclipsed by the Jewish question.

Rogers does not refer to the views of the monarch concerning the *Jew Bill* or its effects.

****

---

[24] French = ordinary citizens.

[25] Equivalent to Guilds.

The Life and Correspondence of Philip Yorke, Earl of Hardwicke, Lord High Chancellor of Great Britain (Vol. 2) by Philip C. Yorke[26].

This work contains the following references to the *Jew Law*.

The Jews' Naturalization Bill received the Chancellor's strong support. It was founded on the clear principles of liberty and justice and was conceived with the object of aiding the development of trade in England and to bring a number of rich Jews to reside amongst us. The Jews had been naturalized in almost all the European states and were among the most useful, peaceful and industrious people in the kingdom. These considerations were overborne by prejudiced popular opinion and a wave of antisemitism swept over the country, bearing down on all common sense before it. The measure raised violent religious, commercial and aristocratic jealousies. The lower and more ignorant clergy declared the Christian faith to be dishonoured and endangered; merchants feared competition in trade, landowners feared dispossession from their estates and the governing class feared that money and not family, might become the passport to power.

The Bill passed without much opposition in the Lords despite the Duke of Bedford's warning that England would become a second Canaan, divided among the Jews. The Bill was attacked furiously in the House of Commons. The Bill was, however, carried despite it being said that, to allow the Jews to settle in England was to rob Englishmen of their birthright as Christians; and that there could be an Ahasuerus

[26] Cambridge University Press in 1913

on the throne and compulsory circumcision would be imposed.[27] Several merchants submitted a petition in favour of the Bill that was countered by the Lord Mayor and the Corporation of the City. Outside parliament, a number of pamphlets appeared in violent abuse of the measure. England would be known as 'little Jewry' and there would be less brawn, ham and bacon sold. The rage of the people was ungovernable. Bishops were attacked and abused. The Bishop of Norwich was mobbed by rude youths who called upon him to circumcise them. The Archbishop of Canterbury[28] wrote to the Chancellor that he was being "a little insulted by the Jews. This ridiculous prejudice is being trumpeted all over England, in which I am not so much concerned for its influence on the next election, as I am to see how easy it is to raise this foolish people to an inhuman and savage spirit, in spite of all the light and moderation which has of late prevailed".

In a letter to the Rev. Thomas Secker, the Bishop of Oxford, dated July 3, 1753, the Lord Chancellor wrote: "Your Lordship knows very well that no one Jew in the world is naturalized by this act, and that it only puts it into the power of the legislature to receive Bills hereafter for naturalizing particular Jews by name, which Parliament may refuse or grant as it thinks fit in the circumstances of each case." The letter also includes a discussion on the legal status of the Jews

---

[27] Ahasuerus was a Persian King who sided with the Jews in the Biblical Book of Esther where there is no reference to circumcision. This is an example of antisemitic misinformation and disconnect.

[28] Thomas Herring, (1693–1757)

in England. Reference is made to *William Prynne[29]*, which indicates that his 1656 antisemitic work was still in circulation in 1753.

An indication of general attitudes of Englishmen to Jews can also be gleaned from the fact that even the Chancellor, a staunch supporter, includes the Jews with Mahometans and any other heathens when explaining how extravagant an idea it would be for Jews to be elected to parliament.

****

Additional Letters[30] to the Hon. Philip Yorke.

Extract of a Letter from Dr Birch to the Hon. Philip Yorke. London, June 23, 1753.

"The Post Office has, I presume, transmitted to you a sheet upon the true nature of the Jews' Bill, of which Mr Webb tells me, he designs likewise to give the public a right notion by reprinting it with proper remarks, having obtained Mr Basket's consent, who is the proprietor. The clamour against that Act is now evidently designed to influence the election next year; and the rage of the people is ungovernable. The Bishop of Norwich was insulted for having voted for it, in several parts of his dioceses whither he went to confirm; the boys at Ipswich in particular calling out to him for

---

[29] William Prynne (1600–1659) was a rabid antisemite. He was prominent in his opposition to Cromwell's decision to allow the return of Jews to England in 1656.

[30] The Foreign Quarterly Review Vol XXII, 1833, pages 449 and 450

circumcision, and a paper being fixed up to one of the churches that the next day being Saturday, his Lordship would confirm the Jews, and the Christians the day following."

The same to the same, London, October 20, 1753.

"Mr Tucker acquainted me in a letter received yesterday that his friends have advised him to add a second letter. On the other side, there was published this day sennight[31], a pamphlet of an hundred pages in 8vo (sic), sold for sixpence, or distributed gratis, under the title of 'An Answer to the Considerations on the Jews Bill'. It is ascribed to Romaine; and has all the distinguishing characters of that writer's impudence, buffoonery, virulence, and insincerity, it asserts 'that the Jews have no God, no King, no country, and never act upon any higher principle than self-interest; that the present set of... [I presume he means bishops] is the only one since the time of Christ, that would dare countenance so anti-Christian a measure'. It cites with great triumph an anecdote, as it is called, out of Raguenet's 'Histoire d'Oliver Cromwell', of the Jews having sent over several Rabbis to make private inquiry, whether he was not their Messiah; from which Romaine, this pamphleteer, deduces several consequences, particularly that the Jews suppose that the character of their Messiah will be like that of the accomplished villain, Cromwell. The chapter pretending to shew from Scripture authority that we ought to have no commerce with that nation, is not to be matched with that of the Church of Rome for falsification of the doctrine of the New Testament."

---

[31] Equal to a space of seven nights and days, a week

Chapter 3

Prynne, Cromwell and the
Return of the Jews to England

The question of the return of the Jews to England was very much discussed in relation to the *Jew Bill*. No official proclamation expelling them in1290 has been found and there was no official declaration allowing their return. Cromwell tacitly allowed them to resettle. This has raised much argument as to Cromwell's motivation and to the legitimacy of the expulsion of the Jews from, or their return to, England. Many of the Sephardi Jews who settled in England originated from the Island of Jamaica that had become a haven[32] against the Spanish Inquisition; and while much has been written about Manasseh Ben-Israel of Amsterdam and his plea to Cromwell for the return of Jews to England, little has been made of the possible influence on Cromwell of his need to retain the goodwill of the Portuguese Jews of Jamaica. That island had been captured by the British from the Spanish in 1655 as part of the ongoing wars in the Indies.

---

[32] Charles V of Spain ceded Jamaica to the Columbus family in 1536 as part of the settlement of a lawsuit. (Edward Kritzler, Jewish Pirates of the Caribbean – Anchor Books 2008 p. 66 quoting Spanish Jamaica by Padron Morales)

R. Monteth, the French historian, in his *History of the Troubles of Great Britain*[33], suggested that money may have changed hands. He wrote in 1739 that the Jews had offered to pay £500,000 for the privileges they sought, but negotiations were broken off when the Puritans demanded £800,000.[34] John Thurloe,[35] who was First Secretary to Oliver and Richard Cromwell, wrote in 1654 that a Jew of Amsterdam had informed him, for certain, that a petition had been presented to His Highness the Protector to obtain that their nation may be received in England to draw the commerce thither.

Mr *William Northey MP* also thought that money was involved. In the debate on the *Jew Bill* in 1753, he said, "Sir, when I say we should not give away our birthright for nothing, I must suppose that we might sell it for something; and I am warranted in this supposition from what is told us by our histories." He added that the Jews never did obtain the protection or countenance of the Crown, even for living and trading in this kingdom, without a very valuable consideration; and the histories tell that they offered £200,000 to Oliver Cromwell for naturalization. Moreover, he claimed to have heard that they offered a much larger sum both in the reigns of King William and Queen Anne.[36] He could therefore, suppose with reason that they would now give a larger sum than they ever before offered, as the birthright of

---

[33] p. 473

[34] Egan – 1848 The Status of the Jews of England p.25/26)

[35]. A collection of the state papers of John Thurloe, Esq., secretary – Volume 2 by Thomas Birch (page 652)

[36] He does not state when.

Englishmen had become much more valuable, and as the Jews had of late vastly increased in riches as well as numbers in all parts of Europe, especially in this country. He added; "But whatever 1 believe, whatever may be known by some gentlemen in the House, it will not be believed outdoors, that such a signal favour has been granted for nothing. It will be suspected that a large sum has been paid for it, and as this is kept secret, as no part of the sum is to be applied either to the public service, or to the discharge of our national debt, the people outdoors will conclude that though they do not sell, they are sold, which will tend to raise a popular discontent against our present administration, and may tend to raise popular disaffection to the present illustrious family upon the throne."

William Prynne (1600–1659) was a rabid antisemite. He was prominent in his opposition to Cromwell's decision to allow the return of Jews to England in 1656. According to Avrom Saltman, in his book *The Jewish Question in1655, Studies in Prynne's Demurrer,*[37] Prynne has been universally recognised as the father of medieval Anglo-Jewish historiography. He used his position as keeper of records at the Tower of London in 1655, to compile his *Demurrer* in which he lists all the sins ascribed to the Jews that led to their expulsion from England by King Edward I in 1290. According to Prynne, the Jews were "a most rebellious, disobedient, gainsaying, stiff-necked, impenitent, incorrigible, adulterous, whorish, impudent, froward, shameless, perverse, treacherous, revolting, backsliding, idolatrous, wicked, sinful, stubborn, untoward, hard-hearted,

---

[37] Bar Ilan University Press 1995.

hypocritical...people", who after more than 1600 years were still "given up to blind obdurate, obstinate, impenitent stupid heart and spirit, a reprobate sense, a cauterised conscience".

Although Prynne was not successful in preventing the resettlement of the Jews in England, his efforts may have influenced some of the delegates participating in the final meeting of the December 1655 Whitehall Conference on the readmission of the Jews called by Cromwell, that ended without a decision. Saltman notes that written history and the collective memory usually condemn failures to oblivion, but surprisingly, Prynne's antisemitic influence has survived through the centuries.

Further evidence of this is in the unsigned, 31-page pamphlet printed in 1753, that follows in Prynne's footsteps with its own equally lengthy litany of calumnies against the Jews. The title page gives a clear indication of the contents, it reads: "An Historical Treatise concerning Jews and Judaism in England, being a circumstantial narrative of the punishments that people have from time to time undergone in this Kingdom, since the reign of Edward I, with an account of their particular crimes and impieties which occasioned them. Collected from our Historians and ancient established Laws; by which it appears that a Jew has no right to appear in England, without a yellow badge fixed on the upper garment, nor cohabit with a Christian woman, nor bring an action against a Christian, but in the King's name. That Synagogues are to be suppressed, that no Rabbi, on pain of death, is to pervert anyone to Judaism, and that a return of the Jews, after their expulsion renders them incapable of receiving any benefit from our Laws."

Chapter 4

King George II (1683–1760) – King of England from 1727 to 1760

This chapter looks at some of the influences that may have affected the attitude of King George II in relation to Jewish citizens and immigrants in 1753. Much of the following has been gleaned from two recently published books; *George II, Puppet of the Politicians?* by Jeremy Black[38], and *George II* by Andrew C. Thompson[39].

King George II was born in Hanover in 1683 and became King of England in 1727. He was also Ruler of the Hanover Protectorate, where he spent much of his time. His wife Caroline acted as Regent in his absence. He spoke English but, unlike his grandson George III, he did not like to put pen to paper. As a result, there are very few personal papers extant and this has caused problems for historians who have had to rely on third party correspondence to adduce George's character and influence. He did, however, take an active role in governing. He would discuss affairs and give instruction

[38] University of Exeter Press – 2007.

[39] Yale University Press – 2011.

individually to his ministers in what Thompson calls an intensive oral style.

Previous historians had wrongly marginalised this King while emphasising the importance of the 1688 Glorious Revolution, which considerably reduced the powers of the Monarch, by introducing the constitutional monarchy and representative government. But, writes Thompson, it would be a mistake to think that the crown had become completely subservient to its ministers. After the death of his eldest son, heir to the throne, and youngest daughter, Queen of Denmark, both in 1751, King George was in charge of foreign affairs, while the triumvirate of Prime Minister Henry Pelham; his brother, Thomas Pelham-Holles, the Duke of Newcastle, Secretary of State; and Philip Yorke, the Earl of Hardwicke, Lord High Chancellor, were in control of domestic politics.

A measure of the King's involvement and independence can be derived from his difficult decision, after the British naval defeat at Minorca in 1756, to confirm the execution of Admiral Byng. He declined to use his royal prerogative of mercy, despite pleas by the then Prime Minister William Pitt (the elder) and others.

George II had an encyclopaedic knowledge of genealogy and military matters, which helped him to develop and direct foreign policy and he was able to adapt to the differing conditions prevailing in London and Hanover. His detractors have accused him of being stubborn, petulant, routine oriented, mean, quick to anger and slow to praise, boorish, weak and indecisive and some have attributed these failings to his early upbringing. His defenders have noted that he remained calm during crises and that he unostentatiously used his own funds for worthy causes. He retained all his wife's servants after her death in 1737 and he supported the London Foundling Hospital.

People and events that took place in his reign are generally better known than King George II himself who was a warrior. He had the distinction of being the last English King to lead his troops into battle. In 1742, he was in command of the army that defeated the French at the battle of Dettingen in South Germany. In 1746, his army under the command of his son, the Duke of Cumberland, defeated the Catholic Jacobite invading forces led by the Pretender Charles Stuart (Bonnie Prince Charlie), at Culloden Moor in Scotland, thus ending the fight for succession. Later, the military victory by the East India Company forces, headed by Robert Clive at Plassey in 1757, heralded the beginning of wider English rule in India. Although the Anglo-French war in North America was known there as 'King George's War', both General Wolfe and General Montcalm who died from their wounds are the persons best remembered. The English victory at the Battle of Quebec in 1759 led to the dissipation of French power in North America.

The marriage of George's parents was dissolved in 1694 when George was eleven years old. The young George was separated from his mother who was confined for life in the German castle of Ahlden. It is said, however, that he did not see her again, although there was an unsupported rumour that he may once, have tried to visit her. He and his sister were raised by Sophia, their paternal grandmother, the Dowager Electress of Hanover who was named in the 1701 Act of Settlement as Heiress Presumptive to the British Throne. This act also included the injunction that the British monarch must be a British subject and a member of the Church of England.

George was naturalized as a British citizen in 1706 when he was twelve, via the Sophia Naturalization Act.

Although he was under the care of Sophia, he did have contact with his maternal grandmother Eleanore d'Obreuse who came from a noble, but Huguenot[40] background that Sophia did not consider to be of equal social status. Thompson says that efforts were made to minimise the amount of unsupervised time that George spent with Eleanore for fear of what she might say or do. These familial disputations must have had their effect on the character of the young prince.

Other factors would also have influenced the King. He would have been aware that the London Jews had supplied a disproportionate portion of the financial support to his Government during the 1745/46 uprising.[41] The King and his father George I, were embroiled in the *South Sea Bubble* scandal of the 1720s when many investors were misled, causing the price of shares to rise rocket-high and then fall drastically when the truth emerged and the bubble burst. It has been shown[42] that it was the Jewish brokers who finally

---

[40] The Huguenots were the largest Protestant immigrant group in England having fled Catholic persecution in France. They settled in the East End of London before moving to the countryside. Number 19 Princelet Street, Spitalfields, a Huguenot house in London, is today a preserved building housing the Immigrants' Museum with a preserved synagogue in the rear garden.

[41] According to Rogers they had supplied one quarter of the financing.

[42] A knavish people – London Jewry and the Stock Market during the South Sea Bubble – Ann M. Carlos, Karen Maguire and Larry Neal – Business History Vol. 50, No. 6, Nov. 2008, 728–748

stabilised the market, to their own cost, and saved many people, including the Royals, from even more severe losses.

A letter [43] from the Lord Chamberlain, the Duke of Devonshire[44], to Mr Gideon Samson, dated June 13, 1758, politely refusing Samson's request for a Baronetcy shows that the King was anxious not to stir up another public antisemitic outcry such as the one, just five years previous, that had forced the repeal of the *Jew Law*. The full letter reads: "This morning, mentioned to his majesty what you desired about the Baronetship. I acquainted him with the service you had been, in relation to the raising (of) the money and particularly, how much obliged I thought myself to you & urged the zeal you had shewn upon all occasions to serve the public. The King seemed extremely well disposed, spoke very handsomely of you, and said he should have no objection himself to oblige you, but as you was not bred up in the religion of the country, he was afraid it would make a noise and in a time of confusion & public distress, as the present is, he was afraid they would make an ill use of it; and therefore, desired that I inform you in the most civil manner that it was not convenient for him to comply with your request. I flatter myself that you will be persuaded that I have done my best to serve you on this occasion, for I do assure you that nothing would have given

---

[43] This letter is filed in the British Library with Gideon Samson's other correspondence with Duke of Newcastle Ref. Add MSS 32886 f248.

[44] William Cavendish 4th Duke of Devonshire had been First Lord of the Treasury in the Pitt-Devonshire government 1756-1757. He was appointed Lord Chamberlain in 1757 with a seat in the cabinet of the Newcastle ministry. The Lord Chamberlain is a leading officer in the Court.

me greater pleasure than an opportunity of convincing you of the regard of which I am your most ob...serv...Signed, Devonshire. London June 13, 1758." This letter gives further support to the contention that the earlier public outcry was over the Jewish question. It is a clear indication that the King had not expected the public's raucous antisemitic reaction when he signed the 1753 Bill into Law. His reason given in 1758, for refusing the baronetcy—"but as you was not bred up in the religion of the country"—shows that he had learned from his earlier misjudgement of the public mood.

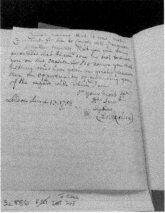

Letter[45] from the Lord Chamberlain, the Duke of Devonshire to Mr Samson Gideon, dated June 13, 1758.

There has been no real attempt to explain why the *Jew Bill* was proposed in the first place, especially when all the

---

[45] This letter is filed in the British Library with Samson Gideon's other correspondence with Duke of Newcastle Ref. Add MSS 32886 f248.

antisemitic arguments that precipitated its repeal were already well-known to the proposers. Rogers says that the concessions in the Bill could be seen to be for political services rendered, a bargain between the ruling dynasty and foreign-born Jews already living in England and he agreed with the *Gentlemen's Magazine* which claimed that the Bill was intended for private purposes, and Endelman claims that the Bill was introduced by the Prime Minister and his brother, as a favour to Salvador and other Jews, a small band of financiers, who had supported the policies of the Government. Robert Liberles[46] opined in an article in 1987, that the hidden motivation behind the enactment of the *Jew Bill* was that "the leaders of the Jewish community sought primarily to enhance the rights of both foreign and native-born Jews in England. And that by securing the right of aliens to own property would, by inference, guarantee the rights of native-born Jews as well".

Still, it remains difficult to understand why the wily governing triumvirate of Prime Minister Henry Pelham; his brother, Secretary of State Thomas Pelham-Holles, the Duke of Newcastle; and Philip Yorke, the Earl of Hardwicke, Lord High Chancellor, would have taken such a politically dangerous responsibility of introducing the Bill as a Government measure, when they were fully aware of the endemic explosive antisemitism extant at the time.

The most likely explanation lies in the King's personal intervention. The Crown, from Feudal times, had an historic duty to protect the Jews, and the Bill of Rights did not remove the King's ability to influence political affairs, and George II took an active role in governing. It would seem reasonable to

---

[46] Jewish History. Vol. 2 No.2 – Fall 1987

suggest that the King, by virtue of his relationship with the Jews and their loyalty to him, as outlined above, asked, or even instructed, his Ministers to promote the Bill that had been requested by Joseph Salvador in his letter of January 14, 1753 to the Duke of Newcastle. That letter has all the appearances of being a subsequent summary of previous discussions. It is too precise to be otherwise. Alas, there is no other written evidence of this, but in all the circumstances, the King's urging and influence would appear to be the logical answer as to why the wily politicians introduced the Bill in the first place; a favour by them to the King.

It is interesting to note that Perry, Endelman, Shapiro and Rogers have all dealt with various aspects of the *Jew Law* but make no mention of the role that King George may have played in its initiation, and contrariwise, the two biographers of the King, Jeremy Black and Andrew C. Thompson, have not, other than as a passing reference, dealt with the *Jew Law*.

Chapter 5

The Jewish Community in Mid-Eighteenth Century London

The majority of Jews in London in 1753 were of Spanish and Portuguese origin otherwise known as Sephardim, having arrived in England via Holland and the Caribbean where they had taken refuge from the Spanish inquisition, which had expelled them from Spain in 1492. At first, the leaders of the Sephardim were the sole official representatives to the British authorities, but later, from 1760, after an increasing number of Jews known as Ashkenazim, had arrived from Germany, Holland and Eastern Europe, the Ashkenazim too formed part of the Jewish Board of Deputies that had been formed as early as 1702.

The leading Jewish personality involved in the promotion of the 1753 *Jew Law* was Joseph Salvador[47] (1716–1786). His parents were Sephardi Jews who had immigrated to England from Holland at the end of the seventeenth century. Joseph was born in England and so did not suffer the restrictions on trade applicable to foreign born citizens. He was a trader in precious stones and metal, exporting and importing to and

---

[47] Also known as Joseph Jessrun Rodrigues.

from India. He played a leading role in the affairs of the Bevis Marks Synagogue, acting at different times as *Parnas*[48]. He became an expert on public finance, an adviser to the Treasury, an important underwriter of Government issues and an adviser to Lord Clive of India.[49]

Salvador wrote to the Duke of Newcastle on January 13, 1753[50], outlining seven reasons why the Naturalization Bill should be enacted. He asked that any person professing the Jewish religion, whom in future it may be thought proper to naturalize, should be able to take oaths of Supremacy and Allegiance or such other oaths as may be appropriate without taking the Holy Sacrament.

Joseph Salvador explained in his letter:

1. *That currently no person professing the Jewish religion could be naturalized in Britain.*
2. *That they could in other countries, thus discouraging immigration.*
3. *That experience shows that foreign countries were attracting the richest Jews from Britain.*
4. *That what was desired was only a qualification for naturalization and then only for those who may be thought worthy and useful.*

---

[48] A Parnas is both a religious leader and community administrator.

[49] Salvador's life and letters are described in detail by Maurice Woolf in Transactions Sessions 1962–1967 Vol. XXI. The Jewish Historical Society of England.

[50] The document in the British Library—Ref. Add MS 33053, ff. 56, is unsigned and seems to be a copperplate handwritten copy of the original letter, which has not been seen.

5. *That the rich Jews have, by experience, shown themselves to be true friends to the Government in every way and with encouragement, will be even more connected as they have no connection or tie with any other Government or state whatsoever.*

6. *That, in any event, as the Constitution now stands, it is impossible to hinder the middling and lower sort of Jews from coming in, and the question now lies as to whether rich Jews ought not to be encouraged, and be highly useful?*

7. *That, as the law now stands, the principal Jews suffer a great hardship, they having sent several Jews to the American plantations, some of whom have returned Naturalized or capable of being so[51], while those who promote them cannot enjoy the like privilege.*

This letter is also revealing, as it shows clearly the desires and fears of the ensconced Sephardi Jews at a time when Ashkenazi Jewish immigration was increasing, partly due to the Empress of Austria issuing a decree in 1744, expelling some 40,000 Ashkenazi Jews from Prague and later from the whole of Bohemia. The decree was not fully executed due to intercession by the British and Dutch Governments.[52]

It is thought that Joseph Salvador also wrote under the pseudonym of *Philo Patriae*, the author of the supportive 68-

---

[51] Under the Plantation Act of 1740.

[52] Moses Hart and Aaron Franks, leaders of the London Ashkenazi Jews were actively involved. (Search out the Land S.J. and J.C. Godfrey – McGill – Queen's University Press 1995)

page pamphlet *Considerations on the Bill[53]*, which sought to rectify the many falsities that had been promulgated in other pamphlets and petitions against the Bill. In particular, he maintained that the Act, that was designed to enable any individual foreign-born Jewish person to apply to Parliament to be naturalized without first receiving the Sacraments of the Lord's Supper, had been totally misrepresented and labelled a General Naturalization Bill for all the Jews far and wide, even in preference to foreign Protestants. No wonder, he said, the public misapprehended the purpose of the Bill. He wrote that the petition that was submitted to parliament, opposing the Bill, confirmed people in their jealousies, and the clamour raised to vindicate the petition had prejudiced the minds of many. He maintained that the Jews were not preferred, they were not even put on equality with Protestants. They would gain no more privileges than they already held and were in fact deprived of existing rights in relation to ecclesiastical livings. He stressed that the whole tenor of the Act was simply to provide a method whereby any foreign Jew, who shall reside in England for three years and could prove his utility to this country, could apply to the legislature to obtain and enjoy the same liberties and immunities as those born in England already enjoy. Parliament was free to approve or reject such an application at will.

---

[53] The full title is Considerations on the Bill to Permit Persons professing the Jewish Religion to be Naturalized by Parliament in Several Letters from a Merchant in Town to his Friend in the Country, Wherein the Motives of all Parties Interested thereto are examined; the Principles of Christianity with Regard to the Admission of Jews are fully discussed; And their Utility in Trade clearly proved. 1753 by Philo Patriae.

He wrote that the City Corporation's petition falsely claimed that the Bill would greatly dishonour the Christian religion, endanger the Constitution and be detrimental to the interests and the trade of the Kingdom in general and the City in particular, and he produced arguments to refute these contentions. In their economic arguments against the Bill, petitioners claimed that Spain and Portugal would take it ill, and that as the number of trading Jews grew, the profits of existing traders would be reduced. Against this, he quoted petitions in favour of the Bill submitted by other City merchants, who asserted that the Bill would actually encourage many persons of wealth and substance to remove with their effects from foreign parts into England, and that they would be gainfully employed in foreign trade and commerce, in increasing shipping and the export of woollen and other British manufactures.

He also denied that there was any truth in the claims that the Jews were a sinful race, or enemies of Christ who would endeavour to make converts. He was concerned that the opposition against the Bill itself, had now become a spirit of oppression against all Jews, both native and foreign. The pamphlet explained that the rule requiring persons to take the sacrament prior to applying for naturalization was enacted in the seventh year of James I (1610) when there were no Jews in the country, and pointed out that Jews had already been given the opportunity to apply for naturalization without receiving the sacrament by the American Colonies Act 1740 (also known as the Plantation Act), so the idea was not new.[54]

---

[54] The Plantation Act states basically that Jews who have resided seven years in any of the American colonies without being absent

In order to prevent Papists or evil-disposed persons from availing themselves of this method of naturalization, the present Bill required that no one shall be naturalized who had not professed Judaism for three years. The applicant must have resided in England for three years without having been absent for three months at one time. The Bill barred naturalized Jews from holding any post of State and from granting any church preferment. They would be admitted as subjects of the realm, but still not with full rights. Had the Jews, as had been claimed, hated Christianity, would they, he asked, have given their full support to the State against the Papist invasion? He claimed that the Jews might even have withdrawn the Bill had the opposition restricted itself to the purpose of the Bill itself, but when the clamour was equally against Jews who were native born, then they found the necessity to continue to promote it. Some, in opposition to the Bill, have said wrongly that it would introduce many poor Jews into the country, and some have said that in their travels, they have heard of several laws specifically against Jews, disingenuously concealing the fact that these same laws affected Christians in the same manner. Some have also said falsely that Jews had to live in a certain district of Amsterdam, and that they could not stay longer than three days in Paris. The *Considerations* pamphlet contains many quotations from the Old and New Testament and its language is mellow, especially when compared with the opposing pamphlets.

---

for more than two months at any one time during this period, may omit the words "upon the true faith of a Christian" when taking the required oaths. (Search out the Land S.J. and J.C. Godfrey – McGill – Queen's University Press 1995)

Joseph Salvador himself, ran into financial difficulties later, and in 1784, he emigrated from London to the American colonies where he lived in primitive conditions until his death in 1786.

The *Bevis Marks Synagogue Records* of the early history of the congregation[55], noted that after the repeal of the *Jew Law*, Jews were not debarred from entering the legal profession because from 1728, they could avoid taking the oaths by availing themselves of the annual Indemnity Acts. But it was not until 1770 that a Jew was admitted as an attorney and no Jew was called to the Bar until 1833.

In 1732, it was alleged in a libellous flysheet that Portuguese Jews in London had murdered a woman in bed with her child by burning them alive. Jews were violently assaulted and in the resultant court case Rex v. Osborn, the King's Bench set a precedent by ruling that a *class* may be criminally libelled. Although Osborn was punished, the ferment continued some six years or more as witnessed by the Synagogue's records that recorded that it was paying an honorarium for 'keeping the rabble quiet' to the City Marshall.

In 1738, Freedom of the City of London was denied to Jewish merchants and traders. This meant that while Jews were allowed to carry on wholesale trade and were allowed a quota of (12) brokers on the Exchange, they were not legally permitted to become retail traders within the City. Even though Gideon Samson had previously succeeded to the Freedom of the Painter Stainer's Company on the death of his

---

[55] BL Vol.4157D1 These are not the original records, but a summarized and opinionated format.

father in 1720 and seven other Jews had received the Freedom of the City between 1687 and 1704, an application by Abraham Rathom to succeed his late father, who was a livery man in the Loriner's Company and Freeman of the City, was refused because the Court ruled that every claimant was required to take the oath on the New Testament, which Rathom had declined to do.

In 1745, in the wake of the Stuart rebellion, the Council of Elders of the Sephardi community, ordered, in the Synagogue, a proclamation of loyal support to King George II and called for the community to subscribe to the Association of Oaths in defence of the realm.

The Elders were warmly in favour of the Naturalization Bill and, in promoting it, they imprudently, against his wishes, mentioned the financier Gideon Samson by name. This occasioned his letter of resignation from the congregation in which he claimed that the elders knew that the matter was directly contrary to his interests. Gideon Samson strongly objected to his name being linked to the idea and he consequently broke off ties with the Jewish community.

Gideon's breach with the Sephardi community was never overtly repaired, but when he died in 1762, he bequeathed a £1,000 to the Bevis Marks Synagogue with a request that he be buried with his people. It was later discovered that from the time of his resignation, he continued secretly to pay a yearly subscription into the synagogue funds under the pseudonym of *Peloni Almoni.*

The passing of the *Jew Bill* aroused a storm of furious public clamour and invective, and in the scurrilous broadsheets and caricatures that poured forth, Gideon, to his chagrin, was often represented as the arch-villain of the piece.

It was said that in losing Gideon, the Congregation lost much, for not only was he a man of outstanding wealth and credit, but he also rendered valuable services to British finances in critical times. He is credited with restoring public credit after the 1720 South Sea Bubble fiasco. He later became financial adviser to the Government and the Duke of Newcastle until his death in 1762. In 1745, when the early successes of Bonnie Prince Charlie caused a panic in the London financial world and a real danger of a run on the Bank of England, Gideon Samson was one of the four prominent City men who helped to restore credit. It is reported that his influence with Sir Robert Walpole enabled him to obtain a special act of Parliament, sanctioning the purchase of an estate.

Gideon's opposition to the *Jew Law* was of little interest to the antisemitic prose and characterization of the time and contra-intuitively, rather than Joseph Salvador, the promoter of the Bill, it was Gideon Samson who received the brunt of the vicious attacks. In various hypothetic and derogatory lampoons, anecdotes and predictions, Shakespeare's Shylock and Gideon Samson were unjustly joined as one and the same.

Chapter 6

Pamphlets

In the period leading up to, during and after, the passing of the *Jew Law*, there was a spate of antisemitic propaganda in the form of pamphlets and letters to the newspapers Over sixty pamphlets were published, and there were large rowdy demonstrations, and meetings in political clubs, and some sixty thousand words were spoken in the two crucial parliamentary debates.

Some of the vitriolic calumnies against the Jews in this period included blaspheming the Name of Christ, cohabiting with and debauching Christian women, defacing the coin of Christendom, betraying national secrets, stealing, crucifying and mangling Christian children and mocking the Crucifixion of the Saviour. It was said that as nature will not allow sheep to associate with wolves, no more will the Law of the Gospel allow Christians to associate with Jews. As locusts are to corn so are Jews to Christians. Only kings and princes and their favourites gained by association with the Jews, while all the commonwealths have suffered by them to excess. The Jews, by their corrupt charms and secret intrigues, boldly presume to engross the principal part of trade, and now they are admitted as sharers in public stocks, and in the East India, African, Hudson Bay and Hamburg Societies. As all the Jews are declared traitors by the Act of 1290, they can call nothing their own. The Jews have taken the Portugal and Barbary trade to themselves and have bid for the Spanish trade. By their remote correspondence with one another, they have driven all the course of our exchange and merchandise before them, and by pretending friendship to all religions, they have got in favour with clergy and laity which gives them many opportunities to drain all Christian countries of their coin.

Some pamphlets claimed that there were but two arguments for the re-admission of the Jews into England, one is the hope of their conversion and the other that the Jews bring in money and promote trade, but MP William Northey introduced payment as a third possibility. In the House of Commons debate, he said that the Jews offered £200,000 to Oliver Cromwell for naturalization and much more in the reigns of King William and Queen Anne. Were we to grant it for nothing, he said, it will not be believed, it will be suspected that a large sum has been paid.

Reference is also made to Millennialism, the belief, from the book of Revelations, that the new-coming of Christ requires all the Jews to be ingathered or spread across the world.

Pamphleteers did not reveal their names but signed off with pseudonyms or initials. Some could be identified by the content. Pamphlets were often detailed and verbose and ran into several editions with adjustments or corrections resulting from opponents' criticisms or second thoughts. Some claimed neutrality. The pamphlets were an important and influential element in the public debate.

The following summaries and paraphrases of various pamphlets, for and against the *Jew Law*, have been kept as brief as possible, while accurately reflecting the messages each intended to convey.

Repetition has been excluded where possible and the language has occasionally been modernised for easier reading while trying to retain the flavour of the atmosphere and heated exchanges of those tense times.

Pamphlet Summaries:

(Against) *A Modest Apology* [56] *for the Citizens and Merchants of London who petitioned the House of Commons against naturalizing the Jews.* [57]

Here are some vitriolic and pejorative epithets taken from this opposition pamphlet. 'Every vagabond Jew may purchase all the liberties and immunities of freeborn Englishmen', 'we look upon Jews who lived in the time of Christ as traitors, rebels against God', 'the present Jews are guilty of the same treason', 'their books are full of the bitterest curses and blasphemies against Christ and they say such shocking things of him as we dare not repeat', 'aider and abettor of regicide', 'The Bill is entirely of a religious nature, it strikes at the very being of Christianity…it is a malignant influence on our religion', 'it is a matter of fact that Jews do live in continuous uneasiness, tormented and haunted like murderers. . . Look at his eyes, don't you see a malignant blackness', 'our God himself told them, ye are of your Father the Devil', 'are these,

---

[56] Currently meaning 'Apologia'

[57] Hebrew University, Jerusalem 1753 Jew Bill Pamphlets and Polemics. (Year 5731 = 1971) 24 Pages. Also found in a booklet published by the Hebrew University, Jerusalem 1971.

the miscreants, the spawn of whom we are going to cherish in our bosom?' 'They who now pretend to be Jews, are blasphemers and shall we naturalize blasphemy? They are the Synagogue of Satan'.

****

(Against) *A Review of the proposed Naturalization of the Jews being a dispassionate enquiry into the present state of the case, with reflections on General Naturalization addressed to: The right Honourable H. P. (Henry Pelham) by J. H. – Merchant*[58].

This is the third edition (corrected and enlarged with several additions) of a 225-page pamphlet containing eleven chapters. The writer believed that no Jew would be naturalized in consequence of the Act, and that the Jews themselves will have the wisdom never to make so absurd a request again. He was against general naturalization and felt the aim should be the introduction of new trades to employ the current unemployed, not the introduction of more foreign workers. There was enough of labour in Ireland where people were being converted to Protestantism. As none of the Jews were husbandmen, manufacturers, mechanics, soldiers or sailors, they of all mankind, had the least title to naturalization. In consequence of their great national crime of

---

[58] Part of the Parkes Collection, Southampton University. Third edition (corrected and enlarged with several additions) of a 225-page opposition pamphlet containing eleven chapters. The title is misleading as this was not a General Naturalization Act.

crucifying the Lord of Life, an unparalleled act of iniquity, the Jews, ought not, and cannot, be naturalized. They cannot acknowledge the Messiah because of their depravity and corruption. They survived the Babylonians, Egyptians, Greeks and the Romans, as it is the will of providence that they be preserved a distinct people, never to be incorporated with other nations. Jews were opposed to all the other nations of the world, but most of all to Christians. Naturalization of Jews is inconsistent with the Christian religion and repugnant to the constitution of Great Britain. There is a great distinction between being passive by suffering Jews to live amongst us and making a law to establish them. So long as they do not do anything injurious to the repose of the State, we have not any natural right to disturb them. Naturalization is unlikely to be of assistance in converting Jews to Christianity. The Bill was first imagined to be entirely independent of religious considerations, but if Christian Dissenters are subject to restrictions, then, even more so, should Jews.

The writer lists the crimes and punishments of the Jews in the past that, he says, prove that they were very wicked and to balance, he also states that the avarice, ignorance and barbarity of manners of our (English) ancestors were not much inferior to the infidelity and immorality of the Jews. He notes how things have changed in their favour since they have returned in relation to the rest of the world. He details expulsions, restrictions and dangers facing Jews in Portugal, Paris, Russia, Bohemia, Austria, Hungary, Italy, Turkey and many other countries. Providence has placed a bar, an impregnable bulwark, against Jews being incorporated with any people under the heavens and in short, the Jews are excluded from everything that can possibly bear the name of naturalization. He mentions *the Usurper* Cromwell and his agreement with Rabbi Menasseh Ben Israel and says that we now see, after hundreds of years of banishment from 1291 to 1655, that the Jews are again established among us, not by law, but by connivance. It was plain to the writer that the indulgence shown to the Jews had hardly any bounds, otherwise they certainly never would have asked for naturalization. He hoped the warmest of their opponents mean them no harm, but we neither love, nor respect them as to endanger our own preservation, or that of our posterity. He dug deep into history quoting King William (1087–1100) and the disputation between the Bishops and the insolent Jews and he warns that the privileges to which the Jews now aspire might hereafter become the chief causes of their persecution. Many knowing ones are already sensible to this and wish to see the Act repealed. If at any time the conduct of the Jews should give offence, their naturalization will raise the higher indignation in the breasts of their persecutors.

He devoted a chapter to the number, employment, riches and poverty of the Jews, the impropriety of their possessing land estates and the absurdity of disposing of church benefices. He said that a denizen is not a natural born subject and he cannot hold lands or legally inherit them by descent and in particular, a Jewish denizen did not enjoy this privilege. He noted that a certain great Jew [59] held his estate by a particular Act of Parliament. This Jew, if we may call him so, brought up his children as Christians. The indulgency of the British Government enabled Jews to acquire great fortunes which they now enjoy safely. May their conduct be such as

---

[59] He is referring to Gideon Samson.

always to entitle them to that enjoyment! Naturalization is improper or unnecessary.

He questioned the estimates of the number of Jews in England. Some said there were only two thousand people, but the Jews have claimed ten thousand. He suggested that there are six to eight thousand, of whom the number of opulent families did not exceed twenty, half of whom were merchants and the number of physicians and brokers hardly exceeded forty. Jewish traders were by no means respectable nor were they considered honourable in their profession, but they were useful in setting other people to work. Then there were the hawkers, pedlars and traffickers in every imaginable commodity and every imaginable way, but very few that could be deemed regular or honourable. There were those who bought and sold stolen goods, and many second-hand goods sold by Jews in Flanders, were of English manufacture. The proportion of their poor must be great and a burden to their nation. They were maintained by the opulent to avoid the pernicious consequences that would arise if they were permitted to beg in the streets as did the Christian poor.

The Jews were naturally or by custom averse to labour. Their religion cut them off and they did not learn the art or practice of manual labour. They were no use in agriculture or manufacture. He admitted one exception, an industrious Jew in Norwich. Jews will not serve in the army or navy and that with naturalization, many poor Jews will flock into England, as they knew that wealth was here, and considering their morals and fertility of invention, they will accumulate enough to pay for naturalization. Some of the expense will be borne by the rich, since for them, the greater the number of Jews, the more will be the influence of Judaism. This Bill does not and cannot confine naturalization only to rich Jews, unless a means test is introduced.

He said that the strongest reason advanced in favour of the Jews was that, as naturalized citizens, they would purchase land and so push up its value and the opulence of the nation. Nothing would be more dangerous. They were useful as merchants but dangerous as landowners. A merchant is inferior to a gentleman of great land estate. There is no immediate danger, but should remote consequences be ignored? Will anyone pretend that land estates would be better in the hands of the Jews? He added that he did not know upon what authority it was said but had been told that a Jew will not fight in defence of a Christian country. It is not consistent in a free country to give a stranger possession of a land estate that he will not defend, although he had been told that in the late rebellion, many Jews were constrained to muster and bear arms themselves. Would there be a grosser absurdity than that a Christian ecclesiastic or teacher, be dependent on a Jew in a Christian country? We might submit to this, if the Jews were to become our masters, but not whilst we are theirs.

Another chapter was devoted to political reasons against naturalization and to the immoral character of the Jews. He sent the Jews a backhanded compliment by saying that it must be acknowledged that there have been illustrious examples of virtue and piety among them, examples that would have placed them in the rank of Christian heroes, had they been inspired by the same glorious principles. It ought to be believed that there were persons of great probity among the Jews in this country. There was one Jewish merchant in particular, he says, whom he had often mentioned with great honour and that person was Benjamin Mendez da Costa, who was one of the warmest opponents to naturalization.

Naturalization of the Jews was not consistent with foreign commercial connections, for if Britain should really naturalize the Jews, a very contemptuous reputation would be created in Portugal, where those who were new Christians, or supposed to be converts to Christianity, were not admitted to any office till evidence was given of purity of blood, after they have passed through above sixty removes since their forbears were known to have been Jews. The ignorant in Portugal sometimes asked now, whether the English were Christians. After naturalization, they will ask, are not the English Jews? When all nations of the world consider the Jews as a separate people, shall we not by naturalization, appear abroad as if we had made our religion subservient to our politics? If Portuguese Jews came to England, they would be received under the protection of the freest and most generous Government in the world. What more do any Jews aspire? And as to those already here, what more than they already enjoy, can they reasonably ask?

There are some who consider that it would be much better for this nation, if there were not a single Jew in it. However, there are several reasons why we should show our good will to merchant Jews, whom we have long treated with indulgence. Whilst the Jews remain Jews, the least return they can make to us, is that of modest deportment. He proposed the removal of The Alien's Duty as an alternative to naturalization.

The last chapter refuted any implied ill intentions of the petitioners against naturalization of the Jews. He wrote that "what was alleged, was expressed with decency and the least appearance of enmity towards the Jews". They were not moved by sinister motives but expressed their fears that injurious impressions would be received abroad. The writer believed that most of the people's voices heard were against the Bill and that differences of opinion were natural, and he called for a cooling of passions. Difference in opinion was no reason for animosity among fellow citizens, as we are thinking men in a Free State. The Jews must be treated with Christian charity.

He also seemed to recant any harsh words he had written, referring in particular to his quote of a pious prelate who had said the infidelity of the Jews should "not be nursed by any injudicious indulgencies which might tempt them to forget themselves". He wrote further, "If any interested advocate for the Jews, or others who are biased by opinion or humanity, should say of me that this man writes as if he repented having appeared against naturalization, I only appeal to what I have written, to the declarations I have always made, if I have not given the least token of indulging any habit of humanity, or want of tenderness for the Jews as my fellow creatures?"

Witness here the dissimulate form of largesse used by the English antisemite that includes denial of any ill will. His Free State is generously prepared to tolerate Jews provided they do not forget themselves and demand too big a move towards equality. Whilst the Jews remain Jews, the least return they can make, is that of modest deportment. He then asks: "Have I ever given the least token of want of tenderness for the Jews as my fellow creatures?"

****

(In Favour[60]) *Further Considerations on the 1753 Act to Permit Persons professing the Jewish Religion to be Naturalized by Parliament*[61] *by Philo Patriae re Second Letter from a Merchant in Town to his Friend in the Country.*

This 100-page pamphlet is in favour of the Bill. It is a follow-up and is designed to be informative about the Jews and Judaism and the relationship with Christianity and speaks of the dangers of anti-Jewish sentiment. The purpose of this letter was to refute the adverse generalities about the Jews contained in the City of London's petition. When referring to the morality of the Jews, it is not as individuals, nor their propensity to certain customs or ways of thinking or acting which they may have imbibed from other nations, but the principles that their religion instructs. All good Christians will avoid denying that the Jewish religion inculcates a true system of morality, lest they give too much room to unbelievers and destruction of the whole system of religion.

Jews are, in their manners, liable to impressions they receive from various nations among whom they reside. Those from Spain have the pride, ostentation and jealousy peculiar to that nation, those from Barbary, the tricking and meanness of that people, those from Holland and Germany, many of the vices of those natives, and, among those of this country may be found many of the English virtues, and more particularly the love of liberty and their country. But they have no power

---

[60] See also further comments in favour, in Jewish Community chapter.

[61] Part of the Parkes Collection, Southampton University.

that may reasonably cause apprehension and their numbers[62] are inconsiderable when compared with the Papists. Nor do they know the use of arms.

With the ascendancy of the Church of Rome, the Jews were reduced to the state of bankers and usurers in most places. They supported themselves with great honour in Spain and most of the eastern countries that received them. The Venetians, the most commercial state of those times (1495), publicly encouraged them. That Spain has suffered since the expulsion of the Jews in 1492, is well-known. Portugal received them but used them worse. France protected them and in 1550, Henry II of France granted them the right to purchase and inherit real estate and Bordeaux flourished. The Grand Dukes of Tuscany naturalized them and gave them power to purchase estates which is why Leghorn flourished. Hamburg did not encourage them, and they moved to Amsterdam where they enjoy equal privileges with the Christians. The utility of introducing rich persons into a State has undeniably proven beneficial to every branch including taxation. The London Royal Exchange is always remarkably thin on a Jewish Holyday. He quotes from Joseph Addison[63] who wrote about the Jews: [64] "They are so disseminated through all the trading parts of the world that they are become the instruments by which most distant nations converse with one another, and by which mankind are knit together in general correspondence. They are like the pegs and nails in

---

[62] About 8,000

[63] An Essay by Richard Braverman in Studies in English Literature 1500-1900. Summer 1994 pp. 537 – 552, gives more detail.

[64] The Spectator No. 495—Sept. 27, 1712.

great building, which though, they but are little valued in themselves, are absolutely necessary to keep the whole frame together." And he quotes Sir Josiah Child[65], who wrote in his Discourse on Trade (1688/90) concerning naturalization of Jews, "Those that are against say that Jews are a subtle people, depriving English merchants of that profit they would otherwise gain, Jews are penurious, living miserably and therefore can and do trade for less profit, and Jews bring no estates but set up with pens and ink only and on becoming rich they carry away their riches to some other country. Those that are for naturalization say the subtler the Jews are, the more they are likely to increase trade, which is beneficial, the thriftier they are, the better example they are as nothing is more conducing to enriching a kingdom than thriftiness and many Jews have brought estates with them and many more would, if they had the same freedom and security in England as they have in Holland and Italy." Sir Josiah Child states that as a principle of nature; all men are alike, and fear is the cause of hatred.

The writer continues at length to defend the Jews in detail and ends on the hidden agenda of those opposing. He says that the only reason for not admitting Jews is that they are already here in sufficient numbers, and everyone knows how close this is to saying we have too many. Judaism is generally taxed with cruelty. Some excuse themselves and say they do not mean to hurt them. Examine closely those insidious writers, see whether (though their outward declarations are such) they do not throw out every reason that could be urged to massacre

---

[65] Well-known English merchant, economist, and governor of the East India Company

them. Are they not in alliance with those who write virulently against them? Is there any other reason for their affected moderation than to attack them in every shape, and inveigle moderate people into their wicked schemes? If they meant honestly, would not their insinuations be attended with proofs? Would they not rely on the laws of their country and on the legislature, without alarming people with false fears? Would they not rather choose some other method to guard against their fears than by their declamations that poison people's minds against the whole legislature, instead of giving the enemies of our religion more room to endanger the State, as they did not many years ago by a rebellion?

Several persons who signed the Merchants' petition against the Bill, were led into it by friends, but were they to consider that some thousands of His Majesty's subjects are unjustly terrified, they might well have weighed the consequences, since as the frog said to the boy in the fable, *what may be play to them, is death to others.*

The two most real and immediate dangers to which we are exposed are the exorbitant influential power of France and Popery. Judaism is a lesser danger than Dissenters of any, or all, denominations. There can be no surer proof of the inability of the Jews to hurt the State, than that in other places, where they are numerous, they are not considered to be dangerous. The consequences of the present clamour and the indecent manner that the legislature has been treated, has produced instances of a spirit of discontent fomented against the Monarch, Parliament and ministers. Such insolence, as to arraign the legislature, can be fatal to the community if none above a Wat Tyler, a Jack Cade or a Massaniello[66], can seriously encourage it. But when we let the party loose without considering the consequences, mischiefs never thought of, arise. Therefore, not as a matter that regards the Jews only, but as a matter that concerns our own and Great Britain's welfare, we should endeavour to allay the present spirit lest bad consequences follow. It is ridiculous to imagine that the present ferment is raised only against the Jews. Think instead of the Jacobites who, as they have not sufficient strength in arms, sow discord and mar every plan formed for our good.

****

(Against) *A Full Answer to a Fallacious Apology, artfully circulated through the Kingdom, in favour of the Naturalization of the Jews, Inscribed to the Lord Mayor, Aldermen and Common-Council of the City of London. By a Christian.*

This 16-page pamphlet is attributed to William Romaine, a leading protagonist against the *Jew Bill*. It was written to justify the City of London petition against the Bill and to show that the uneasiness of many serious and good Christians is not without foundation. Against the claim that restrictions enacted in the year 1610 were only against the Catholics and not the Jews, his answer is that the Act was for the protection of the Christian religion and if it also guards against Judaism then every good Christian should rejoice in it, for are not the

---

[66] Three famous leaders of uprisings.

Jews open and professed enemies of the Holy Christian Religion? Do they not still justify the horrid act of crucifixion?

He maintains that public records disprove the claim that Jews had the right to purchase property. He says that Dr Tovey, in his *Anglia Judaica,* says that while in the time of Henry III, Jews could hold estates, this right was retroactively annulled by a later Act by which such property was returned to the original Christian owners and that future purchases were to be vested in the Crown. Although the original had been lost, a copy of the Act has been preserved in an ancient manuscript in the Bodleian Library.[67] Another Act passed in the time of Edward I, entitled *The Statute of Judaism,* translated by Dr Tovey, banned the Jews from practicing usury under pain of penalties and placed restrictions on the ownership of estates, restricted Jews to reside in cities and boroughs that were the King's own, and decreed that Jews had to wear a yellow badge on their outer garments and needed a special license from the King to sell, buy or rent property. Jews had been given conditional permission to trade with Christians and to purchase houses in the cities and boroughs in which they resided. Some could rent farms for up to 15 years. These concessions were given because the Holy Church had willed that Jews should live and be protected by the King.

The writer denies the claim that foreign Jews would not get more privileges under the Bill than those already enjoyed by British-born Jews, because the Act will permit the unconditional right to ownership of property that Jews do not

---

[67] He reprints the Latin text in full.

currently have. He refers to the popular alarm and says that the public will be even more alarmed when they read what the learned Bishop Kidder[68] wrote in his book, *The Messiah*, an excerpt from which in part says that "the Jews use the most direful execrations imaginable against those who forsake Judaism and embrace Christianity. They teach that such an apostate will have no part in the world to come and will never be forgiven. They spit at him, call his children bastards and his wife polluted and defiled. They curse him three times a day, call him an epicurean and a heretic. They indemnify he who kills him, rejoice in his fall and say woe to his father and mother and his master who taught him".

He disagrees with the 'palliative' suggestion that the Bill only applies to the rich, as there may happen a time when a Judas may be found to betray his master. Nor can he agree that the French example ought to have any weight. His majesty, he says, has shown a dislike for French fashions. The support of their own poor has become a necessary burden upon the Jews, no others being obliged to carry it, and the argument that they have no other country to go to, is not in their favour. Is this not due to a Decree of Providence, and a curse for their persistent obstinacy? As to the assertion that the present uneasiness has been raised only to influence the minds of the electors at the ensuing election, he feels that people ought to be informed of the conduct of their representatives and of the dangerous consequences of this measure so that they can regulate their choice of future representatives so that this Act may prove to be as harmless

---

[68] Richard Kidder (1633–1703) was a noted theologian and, Bishop of Bath and Wells, from 1691 to his death.

as the apologist seemed to suggest, that no one was (and he hoped no one will be) naturalized by it.

****

(Against) *A True State of the Case concerning Good or Evil which the Bill for the Naturalization of the Jews may bring upon Great Britain, by a By-Stander*

This 31-page pamphlet is indicative of the 'neutral' view towards the Jews in general and the Bill in particular. The writer believes that in any case, foreign Jews will not come to England. He criticises the main opponents to the Bill while still treating the Jews with disdain. He complains about language that is not in line with the Scriptures. He decries the unmerciful attitude of a speaker who had declaimed: "Be gone ye accursed race, we will show you no favour." The writer does not deny that the Jews are accursed, but states that to give this as a reason to oppose the Bill is the greatest folly. He complains about another speaker who had declared, "That if they (the Jews) become so numerous and powerful…we may judge from their resentment and cruelty from the Story of Esther which informs us that upon getting power into their hands they put to death in two days, 70,000 of those they were pleased to call their enemies." The writer refutes this insinuation that the Jews were murderers and explains in detail that they acted in justifiable self-defence which any other people would likewise have done.

But it is necessary to read well into the heart of this pamphlet to find this surprising benevolent attitude towards the Jews. For, on the second page, he writes that it is agreed that they are a very subtle and deceitful people and that they are hated and detested by all who profess themselves Christians, whether Papists or Protestants of all denominations. He writes: "Must it not then be the greatest absurdity and inconsistency to suppose that the Jews do not see and know, how detestable the very name Jew is, and that whilst they know themselves to be thus despised, will they leave those countries wherein they now live securely and come and settle among a people, in any number, where they are generally hated and detested?"

****

Chapter 7

Antisemitism

It has made sense to study antisemitism through the prism of the 1753 *Jew Law* controversy when anti-Jew hatred was openly expressed, with no laws to set limits to the form or manner of its expression. Its true nature is clearly revealed in the debates and contemporary pamphlets which were the equivalent of today's social media.

The campaign to repeal the *Jew Law* was the first and prime example of antisemitism being used as a trigger to launch a damaging political attack on the Government of the day. It was used effectively as a weapon to rouse the irrational fears and hatred of the masses. The hubbub and threat of violence created panic in the governing Whig party, whose leadership decided that they had better repeal the Act if they were to restore calm and remain in power.

Antisemitism is dangerous, not only for the Jews but for decent society as a whole, as past and recent history has so clearly demonstrated. It may start with individual attacks against Jews, but if left unchecked, it will become weaponised and used to trigger anti-democratic movements that will threaten the stability of western democratic societies.

It can lay relatively dormant for periods of time, only to be resuscitated when needs must for political, economic or other hidden agendas.

Antisemitism is difficult to define, and though it has long been endured through the ages, and despite many attempts, there is no one single definition that is acceptable to all. There is no good in it. It is evil at work. It is irrational, and yet, it can be weaponised and used *rationally* to achieve, either hidden or open agendas. Antisemitism is more than xenophobia, because its victims are the same worldwide where they are cast in the same mould. It has no limitations and it can be lethal. It poisons the well of decent society. It is amorphous in its nature and can take any form and come from any source. Simplistically, it can start from the dislike of the unlike, facial or cultural, or it can be based on religious prejudice, or political or economic leanings, or just irrational hatred.

Antisemites do not believe that Jews are entitled to unconditional equal rights and opine that they reside under sufferance, wherever they may be. Jews can, at one and the same time be, too religious or irreligious, capitalists or beggars. The truth is irrelevant, myths will do, and half-truths are godsends.

This study of the 1753 *Jew Law* controversy has provided an opportunity to better define this evil concept that is detrimental, not only to Jewish communities, but also to decent democratic societies as a whole, especially when it is weaponised to achieve hidden political agendas.

Current reports show that violent antisemitic incidents in the western world in the twenty-first century have been growing alarmingly, and there are continuous attempts to blur the antisemitic nature of anti-Zionism. Antisemitism and anti-Zionism are one and the same, a mere change of name does not change the intent. Indeed, it is well to remember that the term antisemitism is itself a euphemism for anti-Jew and anything anti-Jewish that was coined in 1879 by Wilhelm Marr, a German publicist. Prior to that date, there was no need for a euphemism to express Jew hatred. There is no basic difference between mediaeval, eighteenth, nineteenth, twentieth or twenty-first century antisemitism. While the language of today's antisemite has tended to be more circumspect, because western society set limits to verbal and graphic incitement, once the mask is lifted, the same basic evil is revealed. This is evident in the development of modern electronic social media, where these restraints have been more than somewhat reduced, or even evaded entirely. That this evil concept is no longer restricted to Christians, does not change its underlying nature, whilst the messenger may change and the method of delivery may change, the antisemitic message remains the same.

On 26 May 2016, the International Holocaust Remembrance Alliance (IHRA), at their Plenary in Bucharest, adopted a *working definition of antisemitism* that has since been adopted by many governments and other institutions, internationally. It reads:

"Antisemitism is a certain perception of Jews, which may be expressed as hatred toward Jews. Rhetorical and physical manifestations of Antisemitism are directed toward Jewish or non-Jewish individuals and/or their property, toward Jewish community institutions and religious facilities." It adds that: "Manifestations might include the targeting of the state of Israel, conceived as a Jewish collectivity. However, criticism of Israel similar to that levelled against any other country cannot be regarded as antisemitic. Antisemitism frequently charges Jews with conspiring to harm humanity, and it is often used to blame Jews for 'why things go wrong'. It is expressed in speech, writing, visual forms and action, and employs sinister stereotypes and negative character traits."

It then provides contemporary examples of antisemitism in public life, the media, schools, the workplace, and in the religious sphere that could assist legal enforcement of existing anti-racist legislation.

This definition is legalistically operational, but it is not fully comprehensive as it excludes the question of unconditional residential rights of Jews and its weaponization to promote hidden agendas.

Historically, Jews may only reside within a hostile society on condition that they behave themselves. This was publicly stated in feudal times and openly expressed in the British parliamentary debates on the rights of Jews in 1753 and 1846 when their landowning rights were strongly disputed. One 1753 pamphleteer wrote that he was generously prepared to tolerate Jews residing in England, provided they did not forget themselves and demand too big a move towards equality, and that whilst the Jews remained Jews, the least return they could do, was to be modest in their deportment.

Jews have been misled to believe that they are residents by right in the democratic countries where they reside. Twentieth century Germany proved otherwise and in the 1940s, the French Vichy Government reneged on the French constitution and expelled many of its Jewish citizens. Other European countries did not protect their Jewish citizens and even British Jews in the Channel Islands were not immune.

By establishing the State of Israel, in 1948, the Jews broke this rule, much to the chagrin of many in the international community. The Arab/Israeli wars of 1948, 1967 and 1973 were supposed to have rectified the 'error' of recognition 'perpetrated' by the United Nations in 1948. The wars failed and the current international Boycott, Disinvestment and Sanctions (BDS) campaign for delegitimising the State of Israel is the latest attempt to put the Jews *'in their place'*, or rather, *'out of their place'*. Anti-Zionists have embraced Goliath and seek to deny David his sling.

Israel has taken the place of "the others" in today's antisemitic vocabulary. The term "You Jews," is the singular incarnation of all Jews into one Jew, when addressing a single Jew, transforming him or her from the singular to the plural, into world-controlling political or financial conspirators, or as the case may be, a collection of subversive communists ready to undermine or destroy democracy or the entire capitalist system, or simply a bunch of cheats, liars or various combinations of the aforesaid.

"Go back to where you come from*"* is another phrase that indicates that as a Jew, *you* are not welcome in the particular location at the time of the instruction. One would think that the speakers know your nationality, as this epithet is usually shouted with outward confidence. However, the yellers often do not know and what is more, they do not care to know, as it makes no difference to them, even if the Jew or Jews in question have the same nationality or place of birth as they have. They just want the Jews gone. This chant has a sinister significance, because it is based on the belief that Jews have no unconditional right to residence, which is the basic antisemitic tenet of mass deportation and, in the case of Nazi

97

Germany, led to the subsequent wholesale elimination of Jews, known as the Holocaust or genocide. The chants, "Jews will not replace us," or, "The Jews, the Jews, we must get rid of the Jews," or variations thereof, have the same connotation.

In pre-Israel days, so-called friendly individuals expressing antisemitic sentiments to individual Jews, would attempt to confirm their best intentions by saying, "It's not you, it's the others," meaning another individual Jew or other groups of Jews unless, of course, the speaker is talking about *you* to someone else. Today, Israel is the "other" that is used to hide the speaker's antisemitic intent by claiming to be a politically acceptable anti-Zionist. As long as you are a Jew who is not part of, or supports, Israel, that exceptional nation, that was established to give permanence to the national aspirations of the Jews and bestow real equality on Jews internationally, then, you are fine; it's not you. Or is it?

The Holocaust was the direct result of institutionalised and weaponised antisemitism and it is a word that antisemites hate almost as much as they hate Jews, although they will refer to it covertly by using such phrases as "Shame that Hitler did not finish the job", or they will insert gas chambers into their shouts as a threatening substitute. They do not like to be reminded that there was such an atrocious happening. Some even deny its occurrence and others minimise the number of victims as though a smaller atrocity should be tolerated or dismissed. Failure to stem Nazi German domestic antisemitism of the 1930s allowed Jew hatred to mutate into the uncalled for and systematic killing of six million Jews and the Second World War. Unrestricted individual Jew hatred can soon become institutionalised. It then allows those in control to use it to their advantage in order to develop their own hidden agendas. Hitler's Nazism is but one extreme example. When society ignores, tolerates or turns a blind eye to, individual or group acts of antisemitism, it leads to institutionalisation. In the case of Nazi Germany, the state encouraged it and became emboldened when the world powers failed to react, or worse, openly denied the German Jews any protection. It also emboldened the tyrant Hitler to promote his hidden agenda that subsequently led to the deaths of tens of millions of innocent non-Jewish civilians.

I have developed my own comprehensive definition:

"Antisemitism is a euphemism for anti-Jew and anti-anything Jewish. It is an evil amorphous concept that can take any form to meet the political and/or social conditions existing at any given time or place. It originated in the false Christian accusation against the Jews of deicide and mutated over the centuries to include the blood libel and false allegations of individual or collective Jewish local, global, political, financial, economic, or media power. It is used as a political tool to divert attention from the hidden agenda of those in power or of power seekers. It falsely attaches detrimental causes to the Jews when the real blame lies elsewhere. It is used to deny the right of residence to Jews, to justify their expulsion from society or country, or their elimination and to deny their right to establish their own independent Jewish Democratic State."

Containing antisemitism or mitigating its effects, requires a positive, rather than a defensive, stance. It is the antisemites who are in the wrong and society needs to know why. Arguing as to whether right-wing or left-wing antisemitism is the more

99

dangerous, is unproductive. Whatever the source, the result remains a dangerous reality, irrespective of its language and the forms it may take. A concerted effort is needed across governments, universities, schools and religious institutions, to explain its invidious nature and to protect society from this evil concept. Antisemitism is sometimes subtle and quiet, and at other times raucous and openly aggressive, but it has never gone away. It is endemic and that is why it can be weaponised for political gain. There is, unfortunately, no simple cure for this disease which must be continuously exposed and confronted.

In his 1753 pamphlet, *Further Considerations,* Philo Patriae noted the dangerous implications contained in hidden agendas. He knowingly wrote "this is not as a matter that regards the Jews only but is a matter that concerns our own and Great Britain's welfare, we should endeavour to allay the present spirit lest bad consequences follow. It is ridiculous to imagine that the present ferment is raised only against the Jews".

It is sad to relate that the antisemitic attitudes, present in mid-eighteenth-century England, that are so well described in numerous pamphlets and voluminous writings relating to the *Jew Law* controversy, are still being actively replicated today.

While antisemitism is openly directed at Jews, past experience has shown that it is a real, if hidden, threat to society as a whole. Unrestricted antisemitism must be seen for what it is, where it can lead, and how it can uncompromisingly damage decent democratic society.

Fin.

CPSIA information can be obtained
at www.ICGtesting.com
Printed in the USA
BVHW091005240122
627018BV00014B/682

9 781398 442276